CELEBRATING 40 YEARS OF THE OPEN ERA

OPEN ERA

40 YEARS

1968 – 2008

The Open Book

Celebrating 40 Years of America's Grand Slam

Edited by Rick Rennert

TRIUMPH
BOOKS

ACKNOWLEDGMENTS

BRINGING TO LIFE A BOOK WITH SO MUCH RICH HISTORY REQUIRES A GREAT DEAL OF TEAMWORK, AND SO THERE ARE A NUMBER OF PEOPLE WITHOUT WHOSE CONTRIBUTIONS THIS BOOK WOULD NOT HAVE BEEN POSSIBLE.

Special thanks to Arlen Kantarian for his guiding, overall vision. Mark Preston and E.J. Crawford gave valuable advice and assistance from the start; as did Michelle Wilson, Tandy O'Donoghue, Jim Curley and Chris Widmaier, and so did Susan Luchars, Brent Stauffer, Beth Meyer and Dan Malasky. A special thank you to Jane Brown Grimes, Gordon Smith and the USTA leadership for their support.

James Martin, Jeff Williams and David Rosenberg at *TENNIS* are owed a debt of gratitude for generously making so much material available.

This book would not have been possible without the tireless efforts of the sport's many photographers, especially Carrie Boretz, Melchior DeGiacomo, Bob and David Kenas, Fred and Susan Mullane and Art Seitz.

Thanks to Wagner | Donovan Design for their design work.

Like Jimmy Connors chasing down a drop shot, Fred Koster relentlessly pursued the production of the DVD.

And last, but not least, aces to Mitch Rogatz and his winning team at Triumph.

Publisher's Note

This book would not have been possible without the vision and hard work of Rick Rennert—thank you!

Design by Wagner | Donovan Design, Inc., Chicago, Illinois

Text by Mark Preston, E.J. Crawford and Rick Rennert

PHOTO CREDITS *Front cover (left to right):* Allsport UK/Allsport, Stephen Szurlej/TENNIS, Fred Mullane/Camerawork USA, AP Images/Mark Lennihan, Matthew Stockman /Getty Images

Pages 2-3: Matthew Stockman/Getty Images. *Page 4* (clockwise from top left): Getty Images; AP Images/Kathy Willens; Timothy A. Clary/AFP/Getty Images; Stephen Szurlej/TENNIS; AP Images/Amy Sancetta; Michael Hickey/WireImage.com. *Page 9:* Jonathan Exley

Back cover (clockwise from left): Clive Brunskill/Getty Images, Shaun Botterill/Allsport, Jon Gordon/Getty Images, Stan Honda/AFP/Getty Images, Trevor Jones/Getty Images, AP Images/Marty Lederhandler, Timothy A. Clary/AFP/Getty Images, Trevor Jones/Getty Images, Fred Mullane/Camerawork USA

CONTENTS

Arthur Ashe Stadium, 2005. *Getty Images*

John McEnroe, 1984. *Fred Mullane/Camerawork USA*

FOREWORD

by Billie Jean King

Over the last 40 years, we have seen tennis grow from the quiet, staid traditions of the sport's famous past, to the energetic, star-driven, power sport of today. Looking back, tennis—at least tennis as we know it today—took a giant leap forward in 1968 with the introduction of the Open era.

We held the future of tennis in our hands and we didn't want to drop the ball.

The advent of Open tennis in 1968 forever changed our sport. Over the years, the United States Tennis Association (which was known as the United States Lawn Tennis Association until 1975) and the US Open took a leadership position and launched what has grown into four decades of innovations and improvements to tennis.

The Open era of tennis unlocked a door of opportunity for all professional tennis players. Not only did we now have a chance to earn money doing what we loved, it brought us together and repositioned us as both athletes and entertainers. Beginning in 1968, the size of the crowds at tournaments increased and tennis was on an upswing. While this new era of tennis was welcomed by players and fans alike, we all wanted more, and thus began one of the greatest moments in tennis history. . . .

If you look back at the improvements to tennis that were first introduced at the US Open, the list is staggering. For example, in 1973 the US Open became the first of the four major tournaments to offer equal prize money for women and men. Equal prize money was about so much more than men and women—it was about doing the right thing. To put this issue in perspective, the Australian Open did not fully commit to equal prize money until 28 years later, and it was not until 34 years later that the final two Grand Slam tournaments stepped up to provide equal prize money.

And the lists of "firsts" at the US Open didn't stop there. Tie-breaks were introduced in 1970, night tennis lit up New York in 1975 and in 1978 the US Open moved to hard courts—after playing on grass until 1975 and then switching to clay for three years.

Through the years, the television package grew larger and larger, bringing the US Open to more and more people around the globe. In 2001, the first Grand Slam final was aired in prime time. And what a match it was. Tennis had done it again—delivering a match for the ages. It was fitting that it was a women's match featuring Venus and Serena Williams—two of the sport's biggest stars under the brightest lights on the sports' grandest stage.

In 2006, the US Open broke new ground with the introduction of electronic line calling. Indeed, so many advancements have been made, we can't wait for what lies ahead.

The last 40 years of tennis have brought us great moments in history, lasting memories and introduced us to our stars of tomorrow. Let this book put a spotlight on the great things from our past and be a beacon for our future.

Billie Jean King

Jimmy Connors, 1982. *Carrie Boretz*

CITIZEN 8:40

OLYMPUS

Martina Navratilova, 1975. *AP Images/Suzanne Vlamis*

Billie Jean King, 1968. *Art Seitz*

13

INTRODUCTION

ON A SPARKLING, LATE-SUMMER DAY in 1968, Arthur Ashe drove a forehand volley past Tom Okker on his first match point to win the men's singles title in five sets at the very first US Open. Ashe collected the silver championship trophy—but not the $14,000 top prize, because of his amateur status—and laughed and hugged his father during the presentation ceremony, at which he graciously said he was "grateful that he was able" to win.

Yet Ashe's day was not quite done. Almost an hour after the match ended, he went back on court to complete a doubles semifinal that had been suspended in the fourth set due to darkness the day before. After 16 games, darkness fell again on the West Side Tennis Club in Forest Hills, New York, and halted the match once more. Play was resumed—and finally completed—the following morning, two days after the semifinal began and 42 games after it was stopped a second time, with Ashe and his partner, Andres Gimeno, prevailing, 6-4, 3-6, 4-6, 20-18, 15-13.

That same afternoon, the duo took on Bob Lutz and Stan Smith in the doubles final and fell in 39 games. And with that, the first US Open fortnight, which broke the longstanding barrier that had kept amateurs and professionals from playing against one another in tennis tournaments, came to what would become a typically exciting, exhausting and successful conclusion.

The advent of "open" competition in 1968 changed everything about tennis—and heralded more changes to come. Tie-breaks. Equal prize money. Night tennis. Prime-time finals. Electronic line calling. Buoyed by these innovations, the US Open has evolved over its first four decades into a worldwide showcase for tennis that brings down the curtain on each Grand Slam season with its unique blend of sport and spectacle.

Moving the home of the US Open in 1978 across the borough of Queens, from the serene surroundings of Forest Hills to the 46.5 cement acres of Flushing Meadows, further expanded the US Open's ability to deliver world-class tennis and star-studded entertainment to the masses. Indeed, the USTA Billie Jean King National Tennis Center (the world's largest public tennis facility when not hosting tournament tennis) and its centerpiece, Arthur Ashe Stadium (the world's largest tennis stadium), have enabled the US Open to become the world's best-attended annual sporting event, with nearly three-quarters of a million fans on-site each year.

For the players, the US Open not only provides one of the game's greatest stages but marks their last chance at one of its biggest prizes—a Grand Slam title. Remarkably, over the 40 years that the US Open has been contested, only 40 players—21 men and 19 women—have earned the right to raise the singles championship trophy. The hard courts of Flushing Meadows have a lot to do with that. They are

Pete Sampras and Andre Agassi, 2002. *Gary M. Prior/Getty Images*

Chris Evert, 1983. *Stephen Szulej/TENNIS*

tennis's ultimate proving grounds, and as a result, US Open titles are won exclusively by match-tough, battle-tested champions—the best of the best. Their names read like a *Who's Who in Tennis* to the point that we've gotten to know them on a first-name basis. Jimmy and Chrissie. Pete and Andre. Venus and Serena.

The arrival of Open tennis 40 years ago indisputably helped turn tennis players into household names. It brought the sport's professionals—its biggest stars, its largest personalities—into the game. And then, thanks to the accompanying media exposure, it made it possible for them to blossom into even bigger stars.

And so the US Open has changed appreciably over the last 40 years, evolving from a tennis tournament into a two-week sports and entertainment extravaganza. As such, it bears little resemblance to the tournament started more than one and a quarter centuries ago.

THE FIRST OFFICIAL U.S. NATIONAL CHAMPIONSHIPS were staged at the Casino in Newport, Rhode Island, in August 1881. In previous years, a number of clubs held tennis tournaments purported to be the national championships. In 1880, at least four such tournaments were staged. But the 1881 event was the real deal, staged by the nation's first sports-governing body—the newly formed United States National Lawn Tennis Association (a name that would be shortened in 1975 to the United States Tennis Association, or USTA).

The entry fee was $5.00 per club, which allowed a club to enter four singles players and two doubles teams. Fifty clubs participated.

Star power was certainly not among the trappings for Richard Sears, who was a 19-year-old college student when he captured the very first U.S. Championships singles title. Among the first American players to hit a topspin forehand, Sears went on to win the singles championship seven times in a row and also won the doubles title six times—five of them with his cousin Dr. James Dwight. Dwight taught him the game and is considered the "father of American tennis," but played only one round of doubles in the first U.S. Championships because he was feeling under the weather.

When that first tournament was over, the receipts, as reported by the secretary-treasurer at the association's first annual meeting, totaled $250 against expenses. That left a profit of $4.32, which everyone at the meeting considered to be highly satisfactory.

The first women's singles national championship took place in 1887 at the Philadelphia Cricket Club and was won by a hometown favorite, Ellen Hansell, who was not yet 18. Women's doubles joined the fold two years later. Mixed doubles—the fifth of the major championships that constitute the US Open—began in 1892. In the following years, the five events were contested at nine different locations, most often at the West Side Tennis Club and the Longwood Cricket Club in Boston. All five finally came

Roger Federer, 2005. *Don Emmert/AFP/Getty Images*

together in 1968, at the start of the Open era, when the men's doubles and women's doubles joined the three other championships already being held at Forest Hills.

IN FEBRUARY 1968, THE USLTA, BELIEVING—like its British counterpart—that the time had come to open the sport at the highest level to professionals and amateurs alike, threatened to resign from the game's governing body, the International Lawn Tennis Federation (now the ITF), if it failed to sanction open competition. The following month, on March 30 in Paris, representatives from 47 member nations of the ILTF concurred. They voted unanimously in support of open tennis, subject to certain provisions. One week later, the USLTA resolved to stage four open tournaments (the maximum allowed by the ILTF) during the year, a number soon reduced to two.

Immediately, the question arose as to where the historic initial open tournament in the United States would be held. It was never a sure thing that New York would be the home of the US Open, although Forest Hills headed the list. The West Side Tennis Club had the longest history of hosting the U.S. National Championships; except for a three-year gap in the early 1920s, the men's singles championships had been played there since 1915, and the women's singles had been in residence since 1921. Longwood was also a leading candidate because it had often staged the doubles and had been the site of the U.S. professional championships for the previous five years. Other cities bidding to host the inaugural open were Boston, Cleveland, Los Angeles and Milwaukee.

But Forest Hills had the inside track. With the help of sponsors, it was able to raise $100,000 in prize money, a much higher sum than Longwood's $40,000. (Wimbledon, the first open tournament to draw every major player, had awarded $62,500.) And with its 13,500-seat concrete-horseshoe stadium, Forest Hills clearly boasted the facilities to conduct a big-time tennis event.

The world's first open tennis tournament, the British Hard Court Championships, was held in Bournemouth, England, in late April 1968, and it proved to be an enormous success. Several weeks later, large crowds thronged the first French Open Championships in early June. And for the first Open Wimbledon in late June, ticket applications totaled four times above normal.

Next came the US Open's initial turn. It was played at Forest Hills from August 29 to September 10, and fan interest was high, drawing a then-record attendance of 97,000—nearly a 15 percent increase over the 1967 tournament. The media coverage was unprecedented as well, while the box office receipts (not counting the income from television, concessions and parking) approached $400,000—more than double the previous year's gross receipts. Most notably, with top amateur and professional players competing against each other at the same event, the US Open finally gave fans what they had been longing to see: the best possible tennis under full tournament conditions.

Forty spectacular years later, the US Open continues to showcase the sport of tennis at its very best.

Venus and Serena Williams, Bob and Mike Bryan, 2004. *Getty Images*

Arthur Ashe, 1980. *Carrie Boretz*

18

Maria Sharapova, 2006. *AP Images/Dima Gavrysh*

40 Years

Bjorn Borg and John McEnroe, 1981. *AP Images/Ron Frehm*

Roger Federer, 2007. *Getty Images*

Grandstand fans, 2005. *Al Bello/Getty Images*

Arthur Ashe, 1965. *Bob Gomel/Time & Life Pictures/Getty Images*

FOR THE TIMES THEY ARE A-CHANGIN'

IT WAS A TIME of revolution; an era that turned the United States upside down and inside out. The late 1960s were a time in which the country was torn by war, tested by political and social strife and taken over (and sometimes under) by the irresistible force of change that slammed hard against its population at every turn. As the guy with the harmonica so brilliantly noted, the times were a-changing.

It was against that backdrop of unrest and revolution that a most revolutionary thing happened in tennis—the sport threw open its doors to professional players, ushering in a new era of "Open" tennis. In the late summer of 1968, the U.S. National Championships segued somewhat uneasily into the US Open—and nothing has been the same since.

It is fitting, somehow, in that summer in which the country often seemed upside down, that this event, now featuring a host of outstanding professionals, would be won by an amateur. And so it was that U.S. Army Lt. Arthur R. Ashe Jr., on leave from West Point, would capture the very first US Open. An African-American Army lieutenant standing alone—higher than the rest—at the end of this tournament's first fortnight of open admission. It was at once perfectly crazy—and crazily perfect.

That first year set the tone for an event—and a sport—that would come to be known for both evolution and revolution. A new era was dawning. Change was coming. It would be slow—painfully slow in some instances—but it would come, nonetheless. An elite sport was becoming much more egalitarian; a tennis championship was becoming much more of an event. The players who contested this sport were becoming celebrities, bigger-than-life personalities whose respective personas positively surged off the playing field: Ashe, Laver, King, Court.

The US Open had arrived. A wild ride was just beginning.

the CHAMPIONS

	Men's Singles	Women's Singles
1968	Arthur Ashe	Virginia Wade
1969	Rod Laver	Margaret Smith Court

Points in Time

1968 WOMEN'S FINAL

Virginia Wade d. Billie Jean King, 6-4, 6-2

Taking the court as darkness was about to settle in at 5:35 p.m., sixth-seeded Virginia Wade overwhelmed top-seeded and defending champion Billie Jean King in only 45 minutes. The loss proved a minor setback for King, who won US Open singles titles in 1971, 1973 and 1974, but the victory was Wade's only US Open crown. In fact, no British man or woman after Wade appeared in a US Open final for nearly 30 years, until Greg Rusedski in 1997.

1969 MEN'S SEMIFINALS

Tony Roche d. John Newcombe, 3-6, 6-4, 4-6, 6-3, 8-6

On a hot afternoon, second-seeded John Newcombe (left) saw his string of marathon matches come to an end at the hands of his doubles partner, Tony Roche, with the match really catching fire in a lengthy fifth set. To reach the semifinals, Newcombe defeated Marty Riessen in the fourth round, 4-6, 6-3, 6-4, 25-23, and Fred Stolle in the quarterfinals, 7-9, 3-6, 6-1, 6-4, 13-11. All told, Newcombe played an astonishing total of 195 games—an average of 14 games per set—in the three matches. His run would prove to be the last of its kind, as the US Open introduced the tie-break the following year.

the HIGHLIGHTS

1968   The five major events that comprise the U.S. National Championships/US Open finally come together at the West Side Tennis Club in Forest Hills, N.Y. ● Billie Jean King plays the first stadium match at the US Open, defeating Long Island dentist and alternate player Dr. Vija Vuskains, 6-1, 6-0. ● Virginia Wade upsets top-seeded Billie Jean King, 6-4, 6-4, to win the first "Open" U.S. women's singles title. ● Arthur Ashe wins the first "Open" men's singles crown, defeating Tom Okker, 14-12, 5-7, 6-3, 3-6, 6-3, in the final. Because of his amateur status, the 25-year-old Ashe was ineligible to receive the $14,000 first prize. Instead, he collects only his $20 per diem. ● With Ashe becoming the first African-American to win the men's singles title at a Grand Slam event, *The New York Times* called his victory "the most notable achievement made in the sport by a Negro male athlete."

SETS AND THE CITY

The US Open and the city of New York share a special relationship that dates back to 1915, when the West Side Tennis Club in Forest Hills, N.Y., first hosted the U.S. National Championships—the precursor of the US Open—in men's singles.

That first tournament in New York was an instant success. "The externals and business side of the tournament surpassed anything ever attempted in this or any country," reported Wright and Ditson's *Lawn Tennis Guide*. As it turns out, the US Open has enjoyed a longer association with the city of the New York than a number of New York City institutions, including:

1923 Yankee Stadium

1929 Museum of Modern Art

1931 Empire State Building

1932 Radio City Music Hall

1947 Tony Awards

1959 Solomon R. Guggenheim Museum

1964 Shea Stadium

1966 Metropolitan Opera House

1968 Madison Square Garden

Marathon Men It lasted five hours and five minutes of playing time, but on Opening Day of the 1969 US Open it took exactly 100 games for 19-year-old F. D. Robbins of Salt Lake City to edge out Dick Dell, younger brother of U.S. Davis Cup captain Donald Dell, by a marathon score of 22-20, 9-7, 6-8, 8-10, 6-4. That remains the most games in a match in US Open history.

Coincidentally, Dick Dell participated in the longest match ever—149 games—in the second round at the Newport Casino in 1967. That time, however, he came out on top, teaming with Dick Leach to defeat Len Schloss and Tom Mozur, 3-6, 49-47, 22-20, in a doubles match that lasted more than six hours.

First US Open Graces Forest Hills
THE DREAM BECOMES REALITY

For more than 40 years American tennis followers and players have talked about the possibility of open tennis. They've argued, pleaded, theorized, condemned and cheered the concept. Most wanted it, and now, at the climax of the 1968 season, they are getting the first US Open tennis championship at the game's American showplace—Forest Hills.

At last the dream has become a reality. Homogenization of professionals and amateurs is here, on the grass of the West Side Tennis Club where the Nationals has been played since 1915.

The line of American champions, begun in 1881 by a four-square amateur from Boston named Dick Sears, is now ready to accept a card-carrying professional such as an Australian named Rod Laver, the man who won the first open Wimbledon in July.

Money is no longer a matter of speculation. It's out in the clear: $100,000 in prizes...

PRIZE MONEY MILESTONES
SINGLES CHAMPIONS

Year	Total	Men	Women	The Spin
1968	$100,000	$14,000	$6,000	The richest tournament in tennis history.
1973	$227,200	$25,000	$25,000	Equal prize money for men and women.
1978	$552,480	$38,000	$38,000	Total prize money exceeds $500,000 for first time.
1981	$1,004,700	$66,000	$66,000	Total prize money exceeds $1 million for first time.
1983	$2,001,000	$120,000	$120,000	Winner's purse tops $100,000 for first time.
1989	$5,124,000	$300,000	$300,000	Total prize money exceeds $5 million for first time.
1992	$8,556,600	$500,000	$500,000	Winner's purse tops $500,000 for first time.
1996	$10,893,890	$600,000	$600,000	Total prize money exceeds $10 million for first time.
2003	$17,074,000	$1,000,000	$1,000,000	Winner's purse tops $1 million for first time.
2005	$19,447,000	$1,100,000	$1,100,000 (+ $1,100,000 bonus)	Kim Clijsters wins US Open and Olympus US Open Series for $2.2 million— the single largest purse in history of women's sports.
2007	$20,831,750	$1,400,000	$1,400,000 (+ $1,000,000 bonus)	Roger Federer wins US Open and Olympus US Open Series for $2.4 million— the largest payout in tennis history.

1969 Persistent rains force the tournament—originally scheduled for 12 days—to be carried over for two additional days. The first major US Open innovation, a huge electronic scoreboard, is installed in the main stadium. John Newcombe and Marty Riessen break the record for most games played in a single set, 48, established only a few days earlier. Vice President Spiro Agnew presents the women's singles championship trophy to Margaret Smith Court (right) after she defeats Nancy Richey, 6-2, 6-2. Rod Laver completes his second Grand Slam and the fourth in tennis history, defeating Tony Roche, 7-9, 6-1, 6-3, 6-2, for the men's singles championship. Because rain delayed the final until Monday, the historic singles final was only viewed by a crowd of 3,708. Soggy weather further delayed the final, which began only after a rented helicopter hovered over the grass court to dry off the playing surface.

FOLLOW THE PROGRAM

Since the start of the US Open, the official tournament magazine has showcased the event from cover to cover.

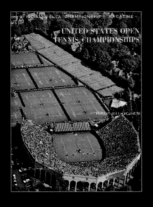

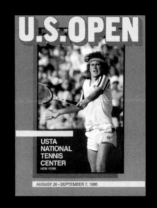

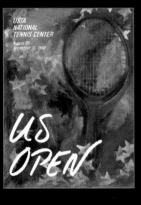

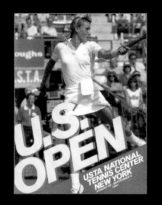

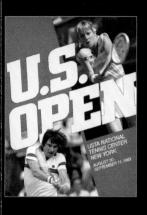

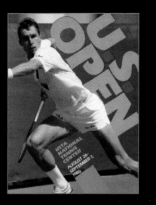

West Side Tennis Club, 1975. *Art Seitz*

BLAZE OF STAR-FIRE LIGHTS UP FOREST HILLS

by F.E. Storer

Eighty-seven years after the first U.S. National Championships were staged at the Casino in Newport, R.I., the US Open on August 29, 1968, was set to open its gates to professionals at the onset of the Open era. F.E. Storer of Tennis U.S.A. *took a look in the September 1968 issue at what was in store for this new age in tennis—and how the professionals would fare against a younger, hungrier generation of players.*

SOMETHING STARTLINGLY NOVEL and different has just been added this year to the staid old West Side Tennis Club in Forest Hills, N.Y., site of the U.S. Nationals since 1915, save for one three-year interim (1921-1923).

For the National amateur singles have been moved away up to Brookline, Mass., to join their brethren, the National doubles, at the Longwood Cricket Club, and in their place the USLTA fathers have decreed that there will be held the first US Open Championships—the long awaited event which most tennis buffs have been dreaming of for lo these many seasons.

Thus, as the ancients knew their year of the locusts, so will this be known as the Year of the Open, when the world of tennis came out of its cocoon to pit amateur against professional in the same tournament. This revolutionary development was brought about, after years of bitter controversy and much political infighting, at the now historic meeting of the International Lawn Tennis Federation held in Paris on March 30 of this year.

Much still remains to be done and there are many questions yet remaining to be answered before the game can be said to have fully adjusted to its exciting new era. What of the anomalous "registered" players, for example, the hybrid created by some of the diehards in the ILTF, which permits a player, providing his home association allows him, to compete for prize money and maintains that does not make him professional as long as he "does not earn his living" playing tennis? Surely, this is semanticism that would make a Philadelphia lawyer wrinkle his brow in perplexity, leading one to hope that this category will die the early death it deserves.

What, too, of the Davis Cup, which has recently been voted to continue to be restricted to amateurs only but which, therefore, will inevitably lose its prestige, since, more and more, the finest players in the world will be professional?

From these few examples it is obvious that the game still has much to do to put its house in order. And yet it has taken the first giant step, and the early results from it are impressive, to say the least. From the first open tournament, which was the British Hard Courts at Bournemouth in April, and continuing right through the French championships to the first Open Wimbledon, the interest has been enormous and the tennis superlative. Bournemouth reported a record gate, Paris had a total of three times its average gate receipts and, while Wimbledon's attendance was down slightly from last year due to the dual effects of a rail slowdown and horrendous weather during the first week, the overall quality of play was probably at an all-time high.

Clearly the Open is good for the game and at long last has put tournament tennis where it should be. And that brings us to the current jamboree that is about to begin, the first US Open. Is it different in any respects from the earlier pioneer opens? Primarily, in the amount of loot that it is offering in prize money to the pros (and a few foreign "registered" players) gathered here.

A total of $100,000 in all is being guaranteed, whereas at Wimbledon the total ante was $62,500. And where Rod Laver took in a $4,800 check for winning the Wimbledon singles, the winner at Forest Hills can earn the grand sum of $14,000. Billie Jean King gained $1,800 for the Wimbledon singles crown; a similar victory here would bring her $6,000. And so on proportionately, all the way down the line . . . ●

Arthur Ashe and Ken Rosewall, 1968. *Art Seitz*

US Open Court of Champions, 2005. *Getty Images*

U.S. CHAMPIONSHI

Helen Wills

Helen Wills

tty Nuthall

Wills Moody

MEN'S & WOMEN'S SINGLES CHAMPIONS

41	Bobby Riggs	Sarah Palfrey Cooke
42	Ted Schroeder	Pauline Betz
43	Joseph Hunt	Pauline Betz
44	Frank Parker	Pauline Betz
45	Frank Parker	Sarah Palfrey Cooke
46	Jack Kramer	Pauline Betz
47	Jack Kramer	Louise Brough
	Pancho Gonzales	Margaret Osborne DuPont
	Pancho Gonzales	Margaret Osborne DuPont
	Larsen	Margaret Osborne DuPont

Louis Armstrong Stadium ramps, 1979. *Carrie Boretz*

Overlooking the Grandstand, 2003. *Al Bello/Getty Images*

Outside a field court, 1984. *Stephen Szurlej/TENNIS*

"MR. COOL" IS OPEN CHAMP!

by F.E. Storer

In 1968, Arthur Ashe won the first US Open of the Open era and became the first African-American to win the men's singles crown. But in the October 1968 issue of Tennis U.S.A. following the first US Open, F.E. Storer remembered Ashe primarily for his talent, his big serve, his style and his class—a true champion in every sense of the word.

FIRST LT. ARTHUR ROBERT ASHE JR., of Richmond, Va., who has been ranked No. 2 in the U.S. for the past three years in a row (1965–67), and who has been knocking on the door of tennis' loftiest level for that length of time, has finally come into his own with a bang.

Starting with the Davis Cup tie at Cleveland against Spain in August—in which he defeated both Manuel Santana and Juan Gisbert in singles—and continuing on to Longwood, where he won the National Amateur Championship, he came into the first US Open Championships, in which was entered almost every top player in the world—amateur and professional—and emerged the triumphant winner.

Arthur Ashe, widely acclaimed in the tennis world as "Mr. Cool," has to be one of the more quixotic players in history. Comporting himself so often nonchalantly, much like a slumbering giant, through a goodly portion of each match, he suddenly awakes and with slashing, thunderbolt strokes, can all but blow his opponent off the court.

This can be extremely disheartening to whoever is playing him, to say the least. Ashe just does not seem to know his own strength.

At 25, he is still developing. And there must be some of the pros who are eyeing his likely accession to their ranks, after he is discharged from the Army next February, with considerable unease.

Arthur's distinction is not only limited to tennis-playing ability, for it was announced at Forest Hills during the Open that Arthur Ashe was the first winner of the new Harold A. Lebair Memorial Trophy.

This trophy, given in honor of the late distinguished treasurer of the USLTA, is to be awarded annually to the player "who by virtue of his or her sportsmanship, conduct on and off the court, and playing of the game, best exemplifies the finest traditions of tennis."

That Arthur Ashe is the first recipient of this award speaks more forcefully of the kind of individual he is than any amount of hyperbole could ever accomplish.

After all the shooting was over, it was clear that the beachhead, which the amateurs originally had opened in the pros' defenses at Wimbledon, has now been widened and firmly established. For a total of 17 pros were defeated by amateurs in singles: 13 in the men's division, four in the women's.

But, most importantly, the fans got what they had waited long years to see—the best possible tennis under full tournament conditions. Clearly, the Open is a great show and a real boon to tennis, restoring the game to where it should be in this country.

Tuesday, September 3. The last match of the day sees fifth-seeded Arthur Ashe of Richmond smash out a convincing straight-set victory over the 31-year-old Australian pro, Roy Emerson, seeded No. 14, who, in his slightly younger days (1961 and 1964), was twice champion here. It is evident from this win that the 25-year-old Army lieutenant is really starting to put together the highly explosive elements of his much-feared game.

Thursday, September 5. Arthur Ashe continues his impressive way with a convincing four-set quarterfinal win in the stadium over Cliff Drysdale in a long but curiously unexciting match. It is ironic that these two should meet here, since earlier this year Ashe had been drawn into a controversy

Arthur Ashe with his father, Arthur Sr., 1968. *AP Images/Marty Lederhandler*

Arthur Ashe, 1968. *AP Images/Dave Pickoff*

over whether he would play in a possible Davis Cup tie against South Africa. Fortunately tennis, and not politics, is the order of the day on this occasion.

Sunday, September 8. The first semifinal in the stadium on this cloudless, sunny day before another announced near-capacity audience of 14,088 is between those two stalwarts of our Davis Cup team—Arthur Ashe and Clark Graebner.

These two amateurs, operating in an apparent sea of professionals, both here and at Wimbledon, have done wonderfully well for themselves, reaching the haven of the semis on both occasions. It is just too bad that they must face each other today, otherwise there might have been the first all-American final here since 1953, but such is the luck of the draw.

They play four sets and just under two hours and, after it is over, Ashe is the winner and, on the day, quite plainly the stronger all-around player of the two.

But, over the course of a match he is a maddeningly uneven player given to some purple patches, at times seemingly indifferent to the business at hand. Such is the case in the first set, which the bespectacled Graebner wins, 6-4, booming in his hard flat serve, one of the biggest in the game today.

But then in the second set, after they have gone 13 games without a break, the Army lieutenant seems to wake up, as he breaks through Graebner in the 14th game for the set with a cross-court backhand pass and a lovely lazy lob that sails over the Ohioan's backhand shoulder for a winner.

Now Ashe is on his way and he takes the next two sets for the match and the right to be ranked No. 1 in the U.S. this year, 7-5, 6-2. Since losing in the National Clay Courts in July, he has now won 25 straight singles matches without a defeat. . . .

Monday, September 9. The men's singles final played before a weekday gathering of some 7,000 fans on this clear, late-summer day with all flags flapping smartly at the stadium rim, is one of the best in the past decade here, going to five sets before the American Arthur Ashe defeats the Hollander Tom Okker (a couple of cool cats), 14-12, 5-7, 6-3, 3-6, 6-3, after two hours and 40 minutes of play.

It is a match that is decided by service—Ashe's—for, although Okker's is effective, it cannot compare to the Virginian's in its awesome power. With that seemingly casual flick of his wrist, the bespectacled Ashe whips down a total of 26 aces, compared to 10 for Okker. And, most importantly, Ashe's serving drastically inhibits Okker's return of serve, which is the main part of the Dutchman's game—to return the ball and make use of his shots.

Tom Okker and Arthur Ashe, 1968. *Authenticated News/Getty Images*

As he did in the quarterfinals this year at Wimbledon, the thin, long-legged American finally just wears down the whippet-thin Okker, who runs after everything and has one of the best topspin forehands in the game today. But Ashe throughout the match supplements his service advantage with strong, whipped ground strokes into which he interpolates some delicate, artful lobs which often leave the Dutchman standing helplessly in the forecourt.

Modest and sporting, Ashe is a worthy champion of this historic first US Open, the first American to win here since Tony Trabert in 1955. And, as the crowd rises to its feet and cheers spontaneously while he is presented with the big trophy by President Robert J. Kelleher of the USLTA, their applause seems to signal not only the end of a splendid match and a job well done, but the beginning of a whole exciting new era in the game. ●

Roger Federer's shoes, 2007. *AP Images/Julie Jacobson*

Serena Williams, 2004. *Clive Brunskill/Getty Images*

Rod Laver, 1969. *David Kennerly/Bettman/CORBIS*

A SLAM'S DAMP DENOUEMENT

by Bud Collins

Rod Laver won the second-ever Grand Slam in men's tennis history in 1962 and then repeated the feat seven years later in capturing the US Open. Bud Collins recalled in the 1989 edition of the US Open tournament magazine how Laver yearned to achieve the first "Open" Grand Slam—and what a treacherous path he faced in making it happen.

"PUT ON YOUR HIGH-HEELED SNEAKERS . . ."

Remember that lyric from Steely Dan's "FM"? Reminds me of a steely man named Laver, who put on his own spike heels (and toes) at a grassy ballroom called Forest Hills. Without that footwear he might not have successfully swirled through the last dance of the magnificent quadrilateral—the Grand Slam.

But with the archaic heels of steel dug in, Rodney George Laver held his ground while holding off another lefty from the Australian bush, Anthony Dalton Roche, to capture the US Open.

"Hardly anybody was using spikes when I came along," says Roche, who at 25 was six years Laver's junior. "Rod had them and knew how to use them. When the referee gave permission for spikes, I stuck with what I knew, sneakers. But they gave him an edge on that wet grass."

Laver was the firebird of tennis, swooping balletically, as brazenly and jarringly as a Stravinsky melody. Derisively nicknamed "Rocket" by the legendary Australian Davis Cup captain, Harry Hopman, the scrawny, poky kid developed strength and speed to live up to the nom de play. His ordinary-looking 5′9″ frame seemed to dangle from a gargantuan left arm.

Rod Laver was something of a jumping jack, covering ground such as no tennis player had done before—or since. His quest was clear: "I wanted the first 'Open' Grand Slam."

Don Budge had showed the way in 1938. Doing the previously undone, the redheaded Californian won the Australian, French, Wimbledon and U.S. singles titles within the year, and the *New York Times'* grand sportswriter, Allison Danzig, dubbed the feat a "Grand Slam."

Twenty-four years later it was time for another redheaded male amateur to duplicate the most difficult of tennis deeds: Laver, in 1962. He was overjoyed to do it. Yet the accomplishment left an itch because Laver knew that—unlike Budge and Maureen Connolly in 1953—he couldn't be regarded as the very best player of the day. Several life-takers named Pancho Gonzalez, Ken Rosewall, Lew Hoad, Barry MacKay, Andres Gimeno, Butch Buchholz and Pancho Segura lurked in the limbo of professionalism beyond the ramparts of amateurism.

"Once I turned pro in '63," says Laver, "I couldn't imagine ever having another chance at a Slam. There wasn't much hope for Open tennis to become a reality in my time. But then the game did go Open in '68, we pros were allowed into the traditional events, and I began thinking about making a Slam with no restrictions. Everybody would play."

It was first a possibility in 1969. The Australian Open of 1968 had occurred prior to the acceptance of the Open principle—the integration of amateurs and pros.

"Once an Open Slam was possible, I set out to get it," says Laver. "It looked to me like '69 would be not only my first chance but my last. I was 31. Rising to your peak at four different times of the year, in different climates and circumstances, is a big order at any age. At 31, well. …"

Slamming, except for Laver II, has been for youths: Budge, 22; Connolly, 18; Laver I, 24; Margaret Court, 28 (1970); Steffi Graf, 19 (1988).

It was no secret, this yen of his for another Grand Slam. But it was a different Slam underfoot from today's: three-quarters grass, one-quarter clay, as ever, in Paris. Since Laver, the grassblades have been supplanted by pavement in America and Australia. Everybody knew Rod lusted for it, and 26 foes had a shot at him. Though they all missed, there were close calls.

Journey's end was the West Side Tennis Club in Forest Hills. A charming enclave with a Tudor-style clubhouse, West Side's grass courts weren't beloved by the nomads of the tour. They were soft, uneven, capricious, made even dicier by heavy rains which closed down the Open for two days.

Rod Laver, 1969. *Art Seitz*

His Aussie mate, and doubles partner, Roy Emerson—three times a final-round obstacle in the 1962 Slam—stood in the way again. Emmo got a good jump, but Laver proved the better bog runner in the four-set quarterfinal.

Then it was Arthur Ashe, with that roaring serve, the defending champion. It was as tense as ever with Ashe, who served for the first set at 5-4. He couldn't make it, nor could he grab a set point against Laver's serve at 8-9 in the third. Darkness sent them home to a restless sleep, the match perhaps far from resolved at 12-12.

A new day and a newer Laver brought it to a sudden end in two games, 8-6, 6-3, 14-12.

More rain preceded the final, delaying the closing of the Slam. Laver and Roche, the country boys from hamlets called Marlborough and Tarcutta, respectively, sat together in the lockerroom talking jocularly with report-ers, waiting for the downpour to cease. Only 4,000 optimistic customers, beneath umbrellas, awaited them in the horseshoe stadium.

Roche said he'd been cheering for the 1962 Slam, but smiled that his role had changed. He'd become challenger, no longer cheerer, and had won five of eight from Laver during the year.

Finally they went out into the dreary, humid Monday afternoon to test their luck in the muck. After Roche dealt better with the greasy court to win the first set, 9-7, Laver asked permission to slip into his high-heeled shoes, the spikes.

"I wanted to start the match in them, but Mike Gibson [the referee] refused. When he said OK," recalls Laver, "it made all the difference."

A pair was on hand for Roche, too, but he felt uncertain about using them.

Ahead by a set, Roche carved out a break point in the opening game of the second. However, Laver sliced a service winner wide to Tony's forehand, and began gavotting in his new pumps to a 7-9, 6-1, 6-2, 6-2 triumph.

Never had a Grand Slam concluded in such a treacherous setting. Neverthe-less, Laver gamely jumping-jacked the net to grasp Roche's hand. It was his 30th straight match win of a spectacular summer. ●

Ivan Lendl and Hana Mandlikova, 1980. *Stephen Szurlej/TENNIS*

Chris Evert and Tracy Austin, 1979. Fred Mullane/Camerawork USA

THE STARS COME OUT

THE WAVE OF CHANGE and challenge that had swelled to epic proportions in the late 1960s crashed mightily upon the new decade, striking with a force that would alter the landscape of the country forever. Civil rights, women's rights and human rights headed the long list of causes for which the caring crusaded. An unpopular war ended; a presidency ended infamously soon after. The country faced its first energy crisis—but never slowed. In short steps and great strides, America moved forward.

The US Open did likewise. As the new decade began, professional tennis was still finding its feet. By the time it ended, the sport was experiencing an explosion of popularity that few sports had ever known.

The brilliance of that explosion helped to illuminate the event to a whole new legion of fans. Indeed, during the 1970s, *Star Wars* played not only on the big screen but also on the big courts of America's Grand Slam. Names such as Billie, Chrissie, Martina, McEnroe, Jimbo, Tracy, Nasty and Bjorn became household names. To fans, it mattered little if they were watching men's tennis or women's tennis—so long as it was tennis.

Fittingly, it was during this era, in 1973, that the US Open became the first of the majors to offer equal prize money to each side of the draw. Tennis was huge—and the US Open became widely known as the place to go to watch the biggest of its stars shine most brilliantly.

By 1978, when the US Open left behind the serene surrounding of Forest Hills for the urban sprawl of Flushing Meadows, a new era of tennis was becoming firmly ensconced. No longer did the US Open—or tennis, for that matter—belong to the country club. It now belonged to the country.

the CHAMPIONS

	MEN'S SINGLES	WOMEN'S SINGLES
1970	Ken Rosewall	Margaret Smith Court
1971	Stan Smith	Billie Jean King
1972	Ilie Nastase	Billie Jean King
1973	John Newcombe	Margaret Smith Court
1974	Jimmy Connors	Billie Jean King
1975	Manuel Orantes	Chris Evert
1976	Jimmy Connors	Chris Evert
1977	Guillermo Vilas	Chris Evert
1978	Jimmy Connors	Chris Evert
1979	John McEnroe	Tracy Austin

Points in Time

1973 WOMEN'S FINAL

Margaret Smith Court d.
Evonne Goolagong, 7-6, 5-7, 6-2

Thirty-one-year-old Margaret Smith Court held off fellow Aussie Evonne Goolagong to claim the last of her five US Open women's singles titles. For Goolagong (left), 22, the loss marked the first of four consecutive runner-up finishes in the women's singles. For Court, the win was the last of her 24 Grand Slam singles titles, the most of any man or woman in tennis history. She would appear just once more at the US Open, falling to Martina Navratilova in the 1975 quarterfinals.

1974 MEN'S FINAL

Jimmy Connors d. Ken Rosewall,
6-1, 6-0, 6-1

The match was labeled as the battle of the ages between Jimmy Connors (left), recently turned 22, and Ken Rosewall, just two months shy of 40. But it quickly turned into the most lopsided men's final in modern Grand Slam history as Connors cruised to the win in a mere 78 minutes. Connors also won the Australian Open and Wimbledon in 1974 but was denied an opportunity at the calendar year Grand Slam when he was banned from the French Open because he had signed a contract to play World Team Tennis.

1979 WOMEN'S FINAL

Tracy Austin d. Chris Evert, 6-4, 6-3

Tracy Austin (left) won her first Grand Slam title and became the youngest US Open champion in history (16 years, 8 months, 28 days) when she defeated top-seeded and four-time defending champion Chris Evert in a surprisingly one-sided final. The loss snapped Evert's 31-match winning streak at the US Open and denied her the chance to break a tie with Helen Jacobs and Molla Bjurstedt for most consecutive U.S. titles. Austin won the US Open once more, in 1981, before her career was cut short by injury.

the HIGHLIGHTS

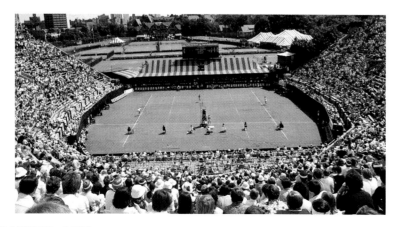

1970 To accommodate increasing attendance, the field-court walkways and grandstand are reconfigured to provide for more spectators. Jimmy Connors plays his first match at the US Open on his 18th birthday, losing to Mark Cox, 6-2, 6-4, 6-2. Top-seeded Margaret Smith Court defeats Rosie Casals, 6-2, 2-6, 6-1, in the women's final to become only the second woman to complete the Grand Slam. Court goes on to win the first triple crown in US Open history by teaming with Judy Dalton to win the women's doubles and Marty Riessen to capture the mixed doubles. Despite playing with a cracked frame in his favorite wood racquet, No. 3 seed Ken Rosewall defeats fourth-seeded Tony Roche, 2-6, 6-4, 7-6, 6-3, for the men's title.

Sudden Death in the Afternoon

In 1970, the US Open introduced the drama and excitement of the tie-break and thus became the first Grand Slam to make use of the "sudden death" method of scoring. The brainchild of Jimmy Van Alen, founder of the International Tennis Hall of Fame, the tie-break eliminated marathon matches and made it possible for spectators to see more matches in a day than was possible in the past. Neil Amdur of *The New York Times* called it "the most revolutionary step in tournament tennis scoring since 'love' became synonymous with losing."

Every time a score reached 6-all, red flags marked "S" and "D" (for "sudden death") were hoisted at Forest Hills to let fans know that tense moments of drama were about to unfold. A total of 26 tie-breaks (the best-of-nine-points) were played on the first day of the 1970 tournament, with Bob McKinley and Ray Ruffels winning their matches in fifth-set tie-breaks.

"They say that on Broadway it's easy to make people laugh, but much harder to make them silent," Arthur Ashe told the media after his 1970 quarterfinal match to John Newcombe ended in a sudden-death tie-break. "Well, in the middle of that last tie-breaker game, the only sound I could hear was your typewriters."

While many people raved that sets—and matches—now had a definite conclusion, some players complained the sudden-death tie-break was unfair, as one player would serve five points and the other four. Five years later, the sudden-death tie-break was replaced at the US Open by the standard 12-point tie-break.

Over the years, a tie-break has decided a US Open singles final only twice: in 1981, when Tracy Austin defeated Martina Navratilova, 1-6, 7-6, 7-6; and in 1985, when Hana Mandlikova needed two tie-breaks to upend Navratilova, 7-6, 1-6, 7-6. The US Open remains the only Grand Slam to employ the tie-break in the decisive final set. ●

1971 Approximately 64 players not accepted directly into the US Open draw compete on New York City public parks courts for four places in the opening round at Forest Hills. ● John Newcombe loses in the first round to eventual finalist Jan Kodes, becoming the first No. 1 seed to lose in the opening round of the U.S. Championships/US Open since 1928. ● Rain delays the conclusion of the tournament by three days. ● Chris Evert makes her US Open debut at age 16 and reaches the semifinals, where she is defeated by the top seed, Billie Jean King, who upends doubles partner and No. 2 seed Rosie Casals in the women's final, 6-4, 7-6. ● Stan Smith, the No. 2 seed, defeats Jan Kodes, 3-6, 6-3, 6-2, 7-6, in the men's final to give the U.S. a sweep of the men's and women's singles titles for the first time in 16 years.

1972 Traditional attire of "tennis whites" is no longer required as the tournament approves pastel colors to be worn by players. ● Top-seeded Billie Jean King becomes the first player to repeat as US Open singles champion, defeating Kerry Melville, 6-3, 7-5, in the women's final. ● Ilie Nastase (left) thwarts Arthur Ashe's bid for a second US Open title, defeating the 1968 champion, 3-6, 6-3, 6-7, 6-4, 6-3, in the men's final, which is viewed by a record crowd of 14,696. Nastase trailed in both the fourth and fifth sets before coming back to defeat Ashe.

UNRIVALED

The semifinals of the 1975 US Open marked the start of the greatest women's rivalry in tournament history, as 20-year-old Chris Evert, the No. 1 seed, faced 18-year-old Martina Navratilova, the No. 3 seed, for the first time. But another drama was soon played out as well.

Tennis officials in Navratilova's homeland of Czechoslovakia were complaining she had become "too Americanized" since her initial appearance at the US Open two years earlier and even tried to prevent her from playing in the 1975 US Open. Navratilova responded to the situation in a surprising way. After falling to Evert in the semifinals, 6-4, 6-4, she went to the Immigration & Naturalization Service office in New York City and applied for political asylum in the United States.

"My goal is to be the No. 1 woman player in the world," explained Navratilova, "and I wasn't being given the opportunity to achieve that."

She achieved her goal three years later—and then held onto the No. 1 ranking for 322 non-consecutive weeks, the second-most of all-time (after Steffi Graf). All told, she won 167 career singles titles, the most of all-time, and 177 career doubles titles. These totals include 18 Grand Slam singles titles and 31 Grand Slam doubles titles—the last title coming in mixed doubles (with Bob Bryan) at the 2006 US Open, when, at age 49, she became the oldest woman to win a Grand Slam title.

the HIGHLIGHTS

1973 Yellow tennis balls are introduced for the benefit of the players, spectators and television viewers. ⬤ On a humid, 95-degree day, 45-year-old Richard ("Pancho") Gonzalez (left) makes his final appearance at Forest Hills, losing in the first round to Tom Okker in straight sets. ⬤ Sixteen-year-old Martina Navratilova makes her US Open debut, falling to Veronica Burton, 5-7, 6-1, 6-3. ⬤ Junior tennis comes of age as Billy Martin wins the inaugural boys' singles title. ⬤ Margaret Smith Court wins her final Grand Slam title, defeating Evonne Goolagong in the women's final, 7-6, 5-7, 6-2. ⬤ John Newcombe avenges his loss to Jan Kodes in the first round of the 1971 US Open by defeating the Wimbledon champion in five sets, 6-4, 1-6, 4-6, 6-2, 6-3, in the men's final.

1974 Grass makes its final appearance as the court surface of the US Open. ⬤ Ilana Kloss claims the inaugural girls' singles title. ⬤ Billie Jean King notches her third US Open title, defeating Evonne Goolagong, 3-6, 6-3, 7-5, in the women's final after the Aussie ended Chris Evert's 56-match winning streak in the semifinals. ⬤ Twenty-two-year-old Jimmy Connors captures his first US Open title by losing only two games to 39-year-old Ken Rosewall, 6-1, 6-0, 6-1, in the most lopsided men's final in tournament history.

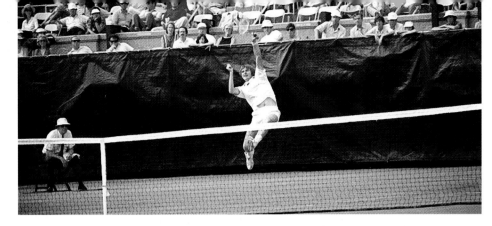

Courting Victory

Jimmy Connors set a mark unlikely to be matched, much less broken, when he dispatched Bjorn Borg in straight sets to win the 1978 US Open men's singles title. He remains the only player, male or female, to win the singles championship on three different surfaces. Connors won twice at the West Side Tennis Club in Forest Hills—on grass in 1974 and on clay (Har-Tru) in 1976—and captured his third championship on hard court (DecoTurf II) in 1978 at the USTA National Tennis Center.

The switch from clay to hard courts in 1978 was not without its detractors. The court surface was faster than a number of players had anticipated, and some of them threatened a boycott, saying the surface favored Americans players. In any event, the hard courts certainly proved comfortable for Connors, who went on to win two more US Open men's singles crowns, in 1982 and 1983.

1975 To ensure quick drying and help eliminate delays due to inclement weather, the courts are switched to a clay-like Har-Tru surface. ● Bjorn Borg ends the Rod Laver era at the US Open, defeating "The Rocket" in the Round of 16 in Laver's final US Open appearance. ● Chris Evert makes the most of the first US Open played on clay courts by defeating Evonne Goolagong, 5-7, 6-4, 6-2, for her first US Open women's singles title. The victory over Goolagong is Evert's 85th in what would become a 125-match winning streak on clay. ● The newly installed lights at the West Side Tennis Club shine on one of the greatest comebacks in tennis history as Manuel Orantes (right) saves five match points and comes back from being down two-sets-to-one and 0-5 in the fourth set to defeat Guillermo Vilas, 4-6, 1-6, 6-2, 7-5, 6-4, in the semifinals. Less than 18 hours later, Orantes upsets top-seeded and defending champion Jimmy Connors, 6-4, 6-3, 6-3, in the men's singles final.

EYES ON THE PRIZE

A landmark was reached in 1973 as the US Open became the first Grand Slam to award equal prize money to men and women. The biggest beneficiaries of the first equal checks were Margaret Smith Court and John Newcombe, who earned $25,000 apiece for their respective singles championships—and were part of the winning women's and men's doubles teams as well. Billie Jean King struck another blow for equality just 12 days after the women's final, defeating Bobby Riggs, 6-4, 6-3, 6-3, in the much-heralded "Battle of the Sexes."

The US Open remained the only Grand Slam event to award equal prize money for nearly 30 years, until the Australian Open followed suit in 2001. The French Open and Wimbledon awarded equal prize money for the first time in 2007. ●

Night Life

The 1975 US Open introduced two major innovations: the courts were switched from grass to clay, and the West Side Tennis Club in Forest Hills was equipped with 48 metal-halide lamps to enable matches to be played at night.

During that first year of night tennis at the US Open, feature matches were presented on eight nights, with the first match taking place on August 27. Only 4,949 fans turned out to watch Onny Parun of New Zealand upset American Stan Smith, the 1971 US Open champion. That night match "didn't seem like that big a deal at the time," recalled Parun.

But now, more than 30 years into the illuminated era of the US Open, the spectacle of players battling under the Arthur Ashe Stadium lights is very much a big deal—and a staple of the tournament. At the 2007 US Open, all 12 night sessions were sold out, with a crowd of 23,757 filling Arthur Ashe Stadium on Opening Night, the largest night crowd in US Open history. ●

the HIGHLIGHTS

1976 Reflecting the beginning of globalization in tennis, for the first time in US Open history no Australian player is seeded. ● Chris Evert wins her second US Open title in a row by defeating Evonne Goolagong in the women's final for the second consecutive year, this time by 6-3, 6-0. ● Jimmy Connors and Bjorn Borg play a memorable men's final highlighted by a 70-minute third set that Connors wins in an 11-9 tie-break after saving four set points. Connors triumphs in the match, 6-4, 3-6, 7-6, 6-4, for his second US Open title.

1977 In the last US Open played at the West Side Tennis Club in Forest Hills, US Open crowds get their first look at Tracy Austin (right) and John McEnroe. Austin, the 14-year-old tennis sensation, upsets No. 4 seed Sue Barker and reaches the quarterfinals. McEnroe, from nearby Douglaston, N.Y., earns three victories before bowing to 1975 US Open champion Manuel Orantes. ● Mike Fishbach's controversial—and eventually outlawed—"spaghetti strings" racquet earns him a second-round upset of Stan Smith. ● Forty-two-year-old transsexual Renee Richards loses in the first round to No. 3 seed Virginia Wade but reaches the doubles final with Bettyann Stuart. ● Chris Evert wins her third straight singles title, defeating Wendy Turnbull in the women's final, 7-6, 6-2, and gains the distinction of being the only woman to win a US Open singles title on clay courts. ● Guillermo Vilas shocks defending champion Jimmy Connors in a dramatic four-set men's final, 2-6, 6-3, 7-5, 6-0.

THE STORM BEFORE THE CALM

In one of the wildest matches in US Open history, two of the more tempestuous players of the Open era, 33-year-old Ilie Nastase and 20-year-old John McEnroe, met on a Thursday night in the second round of the 1979 US Open. The crowd of more than 10,000 was ready for tempers to fly, and that's exactly what happened when chair umpire Frank Hammond ordered McEnroe to serve with the score at 6-4, 4-6, 2-1, as fans were being seated and before Nastase was apparently ready.

"I thought it was a big joke," McEnroe said later. "Then I heard Frank call 15-0 after the serve."

It was no joke, at least not to Nastase. He complained about the "quick serve" and was slapped with a game penalty. When he continued to argue, Hammond defaulted him, and an 18-minute free-for-all ensued. The fans showered the court with protests, upset at having the match end so abruptly.

Tournament referee Mike Blanchard ultimately stepped in and reinstated Nastase, and then replaced Hammond on the chair for the remainder of the match, which McEnroe won in four sets.

The rest of the tournament proceeded without incident for McEnroe. Two of his opponents defaulted in the next three rounds, and in the semifinals he exacted a measure of revenge against defending champion Jimmy Connors, who had knocked out McEnroe in the previous year's semifinals, beating him decisively, 6-3, 6-3, 7-5.

In the championship match, McEnroe (left) faced his close friend Vitas Gerulaitis, (right), who had also grown up in Queens, the borough in which the USTA National Tennis Center is located. However, on this day the two players were miles apart, with McEnroe losing his serve only once, in the first set. He handily defeated Gerulaitis, 7-5, 6-3, 6-3, to calmly take home the first of his four US Open singles titles. ●

1978 Spearheaded by United States Tennis Association President W. E. "Slew" Hester, the US Open moves to the hard courts of the USTA National Tennis Center in Flushing Meadows, N.Y. ● Bjorn Borg and Bob Hewitt play the first match ever on Stadium Court, on Tuesday night, August 29. ● Sixteen-year-old Pam Shriver (right), armed with a 110-square-inch oversized racquet, reaches the women's singles final, where she falls to Chris Evert, 7-5, 6-4. The victory gives Evert her fourth straight US Open title, tying the record set by Molla B. Mallory (1915–18) and Helen H. Jacobs (1932–35). ● Playing in his fifth straight US Open men's final, Jimmy Connors dispatches Bjorn Borg in straight sets, 6-4, 6-2, 6-2, for his third US Open title, each one on a different surface.

1979 Kathy Horvath, five days past her 14th birthday, becomes the youngest woman to play in the US Open, losing in the first round to Dianne Fromholtz, 7-6, 6-2. ● Tracy Austin becomes the youngest US Open champion at the age of 16 years, eight months and 28 days, defeating four-time defending champion Chris Evert Lloyd, 6-4, 6-3, in the women's final. Austin's win breaks Evert Lloyd's 31-match winning streak at the US Open. ● Four Americans reach the men's semifinals for the first time since 1950. It has not happened since. ● John McEnroe claims his first Grand Slam singles title with a 7-5, 6-3, 6-3, victory over Vitas Gerulaitis in the men's final.

Andre Agassi, 1989. *Bob Kenas*

Field court signs, 1983. *Carrie Boretz*

Center court scoreboard, 1979. *Carrie Boretz*

MEN'S SINGLES

Presented by

LEXUS

CHAMPION

US OPEN

Tournament draw board, 2005. *Nick Laham/Getty Images*

THE YEAR OF CHRISSIE AT FOREST HILLS

by Barry Lorge

The 1971 US Open introduced America to its next tennis darling—a player who would charm the crowd as a 16-year-old and develop into one of the greatest American-born tennis players of all time. Barry Lorge of TENNIS *took in the scene and wrote in the November 1971 issue how Chris Evert stole the show at her first US Open.*

TRACY WOODCOCK, AGE EIGHT AND A HALF, is one of those little girls with the face of an angel. Her smile blends in with flowers and blue sky and butterflies, and she wears red shoes that hardly ever seem to touch the ground. She half-runs and half-skips, as if life were just a big game of hopscotch. She's got big, bright eyes that can melt your heart or make you whistle, and when you gaze into them, it's easy to imagine what Chris Evert must have looked like seven and a half years ago, when she was Tracy's age.

It was easy to imagine when you saw them together at Forest Hills, on the terrace of the West Side Tennis Club, where Tracy's father Warren is the pro. They met on the afternoon Chris lost to Billie Jean King in the semifinals of the US Open—the tennis tournament which, everyone agreed, she had turned into a fairy tale.

The match had ended an hour before—the kind of realistic ending you expect from a 20th-century fairy tale—but press and television interviews had dragged on so that Chris was only now reaching the dressing room. Squirming slowly through the crowd, obliging autograph-seekers and well-wishers in numbers usually reserved for a winner, Chris did not notice her shadow: the little girl in red, white and blue, clutching a silk scarf of the same colors, who was following on her heels, lips curled in nervous anticipation of a chance to catch her heroine's attention. Finally, the shadow reached out and gently tugged at Chris's sweater.

"I want you to have this," Tracy whispered, quickly stuffing a scarf into Chris's hand. "Please take it."

Tracy's heart was wrapped up in that gift, and Chris accepted it as tenderly as it was given. "It's beautiful," she said. "You're very thoughtful. ...What's your name?" They talked for a few moments, and Chris said "thank you" again before vanishing into the dressing room.

For about three pulse beats, Tracy was transfixed. Then she burst into tears, turned, and raced down a walkway toward the Stadium. She didn't want the world to see her crying, so she found a solitary corner and buried her head in her hands.

"I wanted her to win so much," Tracy sobbed, trembling as she tried to choke back the tears. "I thought she was going to win. . . . I thought she could. . . . I love her, and I didn't want her to lose."

When you're an eight-and-a-half-year-old girl, sixteen is a very advanced age, and Chris Evert is the kind of girl you'd like to grow up to be.

Three Fantasyland comebacks against tough opponents. Phone calls home to her father-coach in Fort Lauderdale to calmly announce each victory. Crowds which abandon "tennis" decorum to rock an old ballpark with cheers and groans on every point. Groundskeepers who craned their necks and anxiously wondered, "How's she doing?" as they manicured courts away from the center of gravity. Men in elevators downtown who looked up from their newspapers and mumbled, "Hey, that little girl is going to win the tennis tournament."

In the *Times,* she became "Cinderella in Sneakers." In the *Daily News,* "Little Miss Sunshine." And in the hearts of the people at Forest Hills and around the nation, "Chrissie." It would probably still be "Chrissie" even if they knew she considers the "-sie" a little-girl suffix that should be eliminated.

For 10 wonderful, reassuring days, New York was a sentimental place and the US Open was a great romance. Thousands of people have little things—personal things—to remember it by.

Long after the details of the matches are forgotten, someone will say, "I remember the day perfectly. As Chrissie went into the dressing room, a little girl gave her a scarf and then ran away in tears." That is the sort of tableau which sticks in the mind, like the frontispiece of an elegant story-book. It brings back the sequence of events in big Olde English letters.

Chris Evert, 1975. *AP Images/David Pickoff*

Twenty years later, people were recalling September of '51, when Maureen Connolly—three months older than the Chris Evert of 1971—became the youngest champion in Forest Hills history. They were moved at the time, and they remembered the scene in terms of their own feelings.

Twenty years from now people will recall how they celebrated Chris Evert's youth bash. They'll recall her daintily decorated tennis dresses—trimmed in red, orange, blue and green, the matching hair ribbons, the sweater with "L-O-V-E" spelled down one side with a tennis ball for "O." They'll dream back to how she was young but so mature, unorthodox and cool, respectful and yet completely unintimidated by reputations.

She captured the imagination totally. And in thousands of individual memories, Chris will be Sweet 16 again, no matter how she may have changed in the interim.

In that sense—the mental freezing of a great moment which can never actually be reenacted—this was similar to the other great tennis story of 1971: Evonne Goolagong's Wimbledon triumph at age 19. David Gray described that as "the springtime of a great talent," and, after all, great talents have only one springtime. Many summers may follow, but springtime can linger only in memory.

Otherwise the two episodes were as different as their sparkling heroines, who have set the stage for the grand tennis rivalry of the '70s. Evonne is a more natural player, and her fluid, free-spirited, instinctively graceful surge was a better piece of art. But the Chrissie Saga, so suspenseful and against the prevailing odds, was a greater human drama. It was sport manufactured from the fiber of dreams and, perhaps, the springtime of a great personality. ●

Chris Evert, 1971. *Melchior DiGiacomo*

Andy Roddick, 2007. *Emmanuel Dunand/AFP/Getty Images*

Boris Becker, 1990. *Bob Kenas*

Louis Armstrong Stadium, 1983. *Stephen Szurlej/TENNIS*

THE USTA NATIONAL TENNIS CENTER IS BORN

by Ed Fabricius

In 1978, the US Open shifted from the clay courts of the cozy, mannered West Side Tennis Club in Forest Hills, N.Y., to the hard courts of the world's largest public tennis facility—the USTA National Tennis Center in Flushing Meadows. Ed Fabricius recounts in the 1978 US Open tournament magazine how USTA President Slew Hester conceptualized and carried out the transition.

IT IS A COLD JANUARY DAY IN 1977 and W.E. "Slew" Hester, soon-to-be elected president of the United States Tennis Association, is aboard a jet aircraft that is making an approach to New York's LaGuardia Airport. The ground below is covered with several inches of snow, and as Hester looks out the window he is caught with the beauty of the snow-covered land below, Flushing Meadow Park in Queens. The Louis Armstrong Stadium, unused for many years, looms into view and an idea is born.

Hester was coming to New York to meet Martin Lang, New York City Parks Commissioner. The USTA discussions with the West Side Tennis Club concerning a new contract for the US Open Championships had reached an impasse and Hester was wasting no time in seeking alternatives.

The man from Jackson, Mich., is not one to waste time on anything, and as his plane came into New York that day, Hester knew where he wanted to build a new home for the Open, Louis Armstrong Stadium. Thus, everything was set in motion for the accomplishment unmatched by any national governing body of tennis: the building of a vast tennis complex in less than a year.

The idea for the USTA National Tennis Center actually began in the late fall as Hester began to seek alternatives for the Open. He knew the tourney should remain in New York and then hit upon the idea that the park in Queens offered excellent potential. Hester contacted his friend, New Orleans, La., mayor Moon Landrieu, to find out who he could talk to in New York City about building a tennis facility. "Moon had been head of the National Mayors Conference and helped bail New York out of its fiscal problems, so I knew he would put me in touch with the right people. He even indicated that he'd like to see the facility built in New Orleans," recalls Hester, "but I felt we had to stay in New York."

So a meeting was set up with the New York Parks Commissioner and Hester was flying into town to work up an agreement. "Everyone thought we were bluffing, but I knew we weren't," Hester explains, and how right he was.

The land that now composes Flushing Meadow Park has a long and interesting history. It all began in the 1920s as New York's man of imagination, a man who was always thinking ahead, Robert Moses, envisioned a great park. Moses was the man who carried his plan on through the years and finally saw a park built over what many felt was useless wasteland.

For those who have read F. Scott Fitzgerald's *The Great Gatsby* or saw the movie, they will recall the scene where Gatsby and friends stop for gas on the way to Long Island. It is a lonely road in the middle of a dump site. That is the area that now composes Flushing Meadow Park.

Nature had made this land too low for development, but a famed name in New York City history, Fishooks McCarthy from Brooklyn, saw that it was filled in. His Brooklyn Ash Removal Company used exclusive railroad tracks to fill in the marshland.

To Moses this was the perfect spot for his dream. It was 1,346 acres, a Central Park and a half, and was almost precisely at the geographic center of New York. Today, it is probably also the population center of the Big Apple.

The State legislature allotted funds only for the building of Grand Central Parkway. Then the idea of the 1939 World's Fair was born. An investment of 60 million dollars started that famed project on its way.

The Park could never really get going, but in 1946 it was offered as a home to the United Nations. It served as the home for the world body until 1950, when the present site in Manhattan was ready.

In 1959 the idea of another fair took hold and so the Park became the home of the 1964–65 World's Fair. Singer Bowl, now Louis Armstrong Stadium, was built as an exhibition hall.

———————

Things moved rapidly after that January, 1977 meeting between the USTA and the city. The USTA delivered to the city a plot plan of what it was going to do and things were underway.

On May 26, 1977, New York City Mayor Abraham Beame and Hester held a press conference that not only announced the plans but also saw the signing of the agreement between the two groups.

In the agreement, the USTA agreed to spend a minimum of $5,000,000 and would be responsible for the facility's 16 acres of maintenance and security over the 15 years of the lease.

The USTA is allowed to use the facility for its own sponsored events for no more than 60 days each year. When they are not so employed, the courts are available to the public for use, at a fee.

At the signing, Mayor Beame said, "This venture is, perhaps, the most unique in the country between a municipality and an athletic organization. The entire cost of constructing and rehabilitating the facility is being underwritten by the USTA in contrast to most arrangements where municipalities build and maintain stadiums in order to lure sports attractions."

And so, the National Championships have a new home. Contrast the scene here with 1881 when there were 25 entrants for the courts of the Newport Casino in Rhode Island. Spectators were seated on wooden chairs around the courts and there were no photographers or reporters present. Today, many languages are being heard on these grounds as another type of the World's Fair takes place.

The potential of the USTA National Tennis Center is great and certainly does not end, but only begins, with what we see today. ●

Maria Sharapova, 2005. *Action Images/WireImage.com*

1980s

Ivan Lendl and John McEnroe, 1984. *Fred Mullane/Camerawork USA*

THE WORLD'S TOUGHEST TENNIS

America felt pretty good about itself in the 1980s, though the decade often played out in surrealistic tones. A semi-popular actor became a rather popular president. A lot of people spent a lot of time in video game arcades, warding off space invaders or helping frogs across busy highways. People went to Broadway to hear cats sing. We learned that greed was good, and given that, we weren't the least bit shy about wanting our MTV. Indeed, America consumed mass quantities of just about everything it could lay its collective hands on in the 1980s. It was a decade of big hair—and large aspirations.

And if Americans spent most of their time trying to out-do their neighbors, tennis's top talents were likewise engaged in an era of remarkable rivalries. Nowhere did these head-to-head struggles play out with more panache than at the US Open. It was here that John McEnroe chased Bjorn Borg from the game, then turned his attention to Jimmy Connors and, later, Ivan Lendl. Chris Evert and Martina Navratilova would write dramatic story lines worthy of Oscar nominations, their every meeting lifting the profile of women's tennis just that much higher. On a Saturday in 1984, all of these grand players helped the US Open record arguably its greatest day. And as the decade ended, another great talent—Steffi Graf—would score the game's grandest achievement.

To outrival their rivals, Lendl and Navratilova led a new era of supreme fitness among tennis players, and in the heat and humidity of the late-summer Flushing fortnights, their dedication to that cause would pay major dividends. Now, others realized that to achieve similar results, they would need to be similarly committed. It wasn't just the face of the game that was changing, it was its physique.

At once, all realized that to win at Flushing Meadows would take just a little something extra. These rectangular slabs of cement became tennis's ultimate proving grounds. The US Open is, after all, the world's toughest tennis. Only the strong survive.

the CHAMPIONS

	MEN'S SINGLES	WOMEN'S SINGLES
1980	John McEnroe	Chris Evert Lloyd
1981	John McEnroe	Tracy Austin
1982	Jimmy Connors	Chris Evert Lloyd
1983	Jimmy Connors	Martina Navratilova
1984	John McEnroe	Martina Navratilova
1985	Ivan Lendl	Hana Mandlikova
1986	Ivan Lendl	Martina Navratilova
1987	Ivan Lendl	Martina Navratilova
1988	Mats Wilander	Steffi Graf
1989	Boris Becker	Steffi Graf

Points in Time

1985 MEN'S FINAL

Ivan Lendl d. John McEnroe,
7-6, 6-3, 6-4

Having finished as runner-up in the three previous US Open men's finals, Ivan Lendl (left) gained a measure of revenge over arch-rival John McEnroe (middle left) with a barrage of savage ground strokes that consistently kept the defending US Open champion on the defensive. The straight-set victory marked a major turning point in the careers of both players. For Lendl, it was the first of three straight US Open titles and continued an astonishing run in which he reached eight consecutive US Open finals. For McEnroe, it would be the last time he ever appeared in a Grand Slam singles final. ●

1989 MEN'S SECOND ROUND

Boris Becker d. Derrick Rostagno,
1-6, 6-7, 6-3, 7-6, 6-3

Facing his second match point in the fourth-set tie-break, No. 2 seed Boris Becker (left) scrambled to hit a passing shot by a perfectly positioned Derrick Rostagno at the net. The ball hit the net tape and sailed over the racquet of the stunned No. 65–ranked Rostagno for a winner. Becker would go on to take the tie-breaker, the match and eventually his first and only US Open title. "I knew after I survived that match," Becker said following his men's final victory, "that things could only get better for me." ●

1986 WOMEN'S SEMIFINALS

Martina Navratilova d. Steffi Graf, 6-1, 6-7, 7-6

In a match that took more than 24 hours to complete, Martina Navratilova (left) came back from three match points to defeat 17-year-old Steffi Graf, who announced herself as the next great women's champion. Putting on a display of fist-shaking and finger-waving emotion, Navratilova led 4-1 in the first set before the match was delayed a day due to rain. Graf turned the tables the next day and had two match points in the final set but missed both with long forehands. She again held match point at 8-7 in the tie-break; but after she missed a backhand passing shot, Navratilova won the next two points to take the match and, ultimately, the title. The two would meet again in the 1987 final (won by Navratilova) and in 1989 (won by Graf). ●

the HIGHLIGHTS

1980 At the age of 15 years, three months, Andrea Jaeger becomes the youngest US Open semifinalist, defeating Barbara Hallquist in a quarterfinal match viewed by a record crowd of 18,606. ● After taking a three-month sabbatical from tennis earlier in the year, Chris Evert Lloyd avenges her 1979 final-round loss to Tracy Austin in the semifinals and then wins her fifth US Open title in six years, defeating Hana Mandlikova, 5-7, 6-1, 6-1, in the women's final. ● John McEnroe and Jimmy Connors lock horns in one of their greatest US Open matches, with McEnroe edging Connors, 6-4, 5-7, 0-6, 6-3, 7-6, in the men's semifinals. ● Bjorn Borg (left) and John McEnroe stage one of the all-time great US Open men's finals, with McEnroe winning in five sets, 7-6, 6-1, 6-7, 5-7, 6-4, for his second straight US Open title.

TRIPLE THREAT

On the 100th anniversary of the first women's championship, Martina Navratilova swept the women's singles, women's doubles and mixed doubles at the 1987 US Open to become the first woman to capture three titles at the same event since Margaret Smith Court in 1970.

Never losing a set in the women's singles, Navratilova defeated Steffi Graf in the final for the title, teamed with Pam Shriver to win the women's doubles crown and paired with Emilio Sanchez to win the mixed doubles.

Twice, Navratilova came within one point of failing in her quest. During the mixed doubles final—which took place three hours after she had clinched her second title, the women's doubles—she and Sanchez faced two match points before edging Betsy Nagelsen and Paul Annacone in the third-set tie-break, 6-4, 6-7 (6-8), 7-6 (14-12).

"When we went into the breaker, Emilio told me he was very nervous," Navratilova said. "So was I, not just for the match, but the triple. He didn't even know I was going for a triple. And I wasn't going to tell him then."

1981 At the 100th anniversary of U.S. Championships, Americans claim both singles titles and the men's and women's doubles titles. ● At 18, Tracy Austin wins her second US Open title, 1-6, 7-6, 7-6, when Martina Navratilova double faults on match point of the women's final. For Navratilova, who upset Chris Evert Lloyd in the semifinals, it was her first US Open women's singles final. ● John McEnroe (left) defeats Bjorn Borg in the men's final, 4-6, 6-2, 6-4, 6-3, to win his third straight US Open men's singles crown, equaling a feat last achieved by Bill Tilden in 1925. For Borg, the loss is his fourth US Open runner-up finish and his final Grand Slam appearance.

1982 Total tournament prize money exceeds $1 million for the first time. ● Billie Jean King makes her final US Open singles appearance, losing in the first round to Susan Mascarin. ● Pam Shriver's 1-6, 7-6, 6-2 quarterfinal upset of reigning French and Wimbledon champion Navratilova is the match of the tournament on the women's side. An overwhelming favorite for the title and the tournament's top seed, Navratilova leaves the court in tears as her Grand Slam hopes are dashed. ● Chris Evert Lloyd (left) captures the last of her six US Open singles titles, defeating Hana Mandlikova in the women's final, 6-3, 6-1. ● Jimmy Connors returns to the winner's circle, defeating first-time finalist Ivan Lendl in a crowd-pleasing, four-set final. Lendl ends John McEnroe's 26-match US Open win streak in the semifinals.

A Truly Super Saturday

It was a long day's journey into night, and a magnificent journey it was. The day began at 11:07 a.m., with John Newcombe serving to Stan Smith in the men's senior championship. By the time play concluded at 11:14 p.m., tennis fans had been treated to a series of unforgettable matches—two men's semifinals and a women's final—each going the distance, not only in sets but in edge-of-your-seat thrills.

In the first of three classic encounters, Ivan Lendl saved a match point to advance to his third straight US Open final by defeating Pat Cash, 3-6, 6-3, 6-4, 6-7, 7-6. Next, Martina Navratilova captured her second straight US Open singles title, defeating six-time US Open champion Chris Evert Lloyd, 4-6, 6-4, 6-4, in Evert's last of nine US Open women's singles final appearances. John McEnroe and Jimmy Connors wrapped up the day's play, with McEnroe eliminating the two-time defending champion, 6-4, 4-6, 7-5, 4-6, 6-3.

Tony Trabert, who provided commentary for CBS for the entire 12-hour-and-seven-minute broadcast, said, "We kept coming back on the air after each match saying, 'Wow, you can't get much better than that.' And then they did."

the HIGHLIGHTS

1983 Aaron Krickstein, the reigning USTA National Boys' 18 champion, advances to the round of 16 before losing to Yannick Noah. ● No. 16 seed Bill Scanlon shocks top-seeded John McEnroe in the round of 16. ● In her 11th US Open appearance, Martina Navratilova (left) breaks through to win her first US Open women's singles title, routing Chris Evert Lloyd, 6-1, 6-3. ● For the second straight year, Jimmy Connors defeats Ivan Lendl in the men's final, taking the last nine games for a 6-3, 6-7, 7-5, 6-0 victory.

1984 Saturday, September 8—perhaps the greatest single day in tennis history—grabs the headlines as all four matches played on the stadium court are extended to the maximum number of sets. In addition to a senior men's semifinal and two men's semifinals, Martina Navratilova defeats Chris Evert Lloyd in the women's final for the second straight year, 4-6, 6-4, 6-4. ● A day after Super Saturday, the men's final proves anticlimactic as John McEnroe defeats Ivan Lendl in straight sets, 6-3, 6-4, 6-1.

The Rules of the Game

The Rules of the Game John McEnroe and Peter Fleming were the premier doubles team of their era. They posted a sterling record of 14-1 in Davis Cup play, won four Wimbledon titles and advanced to the US Open final four times in five years, winning the title in 1979, 1981 and 1983. After a two-year separation, the duo reunited in 1986 and set their sights on a fourth US Open doubles title.

On the day of their first-round match, McEnroe and Fleming went to McEnroe's parents' home in Cove Neck, N.Y., to practice and have lunch before setting out for their 2:00 match. It was normally a 30-minute drive, but they soon found themselves stuck in traffic on the Long Island Expressway.

Meanwhile, the Grandstand had filled to capacity in anticipation of the match, especially with McEnroe having already lost in the first-round singles. By 2:15, the fans were applauding rhythmically to get the action started. When four players finally emerged from the tunnel leading to the court, loud cheers erupted—and died just as quickly. None of the players were McEnroe and Fleming, whose names were being taken off the scoreboard.

Players must show up for their match within 15 minutes after being summoned by the tournament referee. As it turned out, McEnroe and Fleming arrived at the USTA National Tennis Center five minutes after the deadline and were duly defaulted.

"That's the rules of the game, I guess," said Fleming.

It was the last time the pair ever teamed up at the US Open.

1985 Mary Joe Fernandez, at the age of 14 years and eight days, becomes the youngest player to win a match at the US Open when she defeats Sara Gomer in the first round, 6-1, 6-4. ● Top-seeded John McEnroe prevails in the fifth-set tie-break and avoids a major upset bid by Shlomo Glickstein in the opening round. ● A tornado strikes the USTA National Tennis Center in the late afternoon of August 30, causing serious damage to the grounds, including downed power lines, major flooding and uprooted trees. There is no delay, however, and the tournament resumes in full the next day. ● For Hana Mandlikova (right), her third US Open women's final is a charm as she defeats Martina Navratilova, 7-6, 1-6, 7-6. ● Ivan Lendl breaks through in the men's final to win his first US Open title, defeating John McEnroe, 7-6, 6-3, 6-4. ●

To the Left In 1973, John Newcombe became the fourth right-hander to win the US Open in four years. In 1985, Ivan Lendl took the first of three straight men's singles titles. In between, it was all left-handers. In one of the most striking peculiarities in the US Open records books, a southpaw won every men's singles title from 1974 to 1984, a run of 11 straight championships.

Jimmy Connors started the left-handed run with his title in 1974. In all, Connors won five championships during the 11-year span, with John McEnroe adding four of his own. The two other titles were collected by Manuel Orantes in 1975 and Guillermo Vilas in 1977, both of whom won on the clay courts at the West Side Tennis Club.

The amazing streak of left-handed champions led *TENNIS* magazine to have a psychologist analyze why lefties might have an advantage in the US Open. But in a historical context, the run seems an anomaly. In the 92 years of play leading up to 1974, the tournament had been won by a left-hander a grand total of 13 times. And since 1985, only one lefty (runner-up Greg Rusedski in 1997) has even played for the men's singles crown. ●

A REMARKABLE RUN

In 1982, Ivan Lendl snapped John McEnroe's 26-match winning streak at the US Open to reach his first men's singles final. In doing so, he started a daunting run of excellence not seen at the US Open since Bill Tilden in the 1920s. From 1982 through the remainder of the decade, Lendl reached every title match.

Beaten by Jimmy Connors in 1982 and 1983 and ousted by McEnroe in 1984, Lendl garnered the crown from 1985 to 1987 with victories over McEnroe, Miloslav Mecir (in an all-Czech finals weekend) and Mats Wilander. In 1988 and 1989, he fell in bruising battles to Wilander (in the longest final in the Open era, lasting four hours and 54 minutes) and Boris Becker.

Lendl's relentless pursuit of excellence remains as great an achievement as his remarkable run. Training hard and playing hard year after year, he showed an entire generation of players what it takes to be a champion: determination, commitment and exceptional conditioning. ●

the HIGHLIGHTS

1986 John McEnroe suffers his earliest exit from the US Open, losing in the first round to Paul Annacone, 1-6, 6-1, 6-3, 6-3. ● Andre Agassi makes his US Open debut as a 16-year-old, losing in the first round to Jeremy Bates, 7-6, 6-3, 4-6, 6-4. Agassi will not miss a US Open through his retirement in 2006. ● Jimmy Connors's streak of 12 straight semifinal berths is ended by Todd Witsken in the third round. ● Tim Wilkison is the lone American man to reach the quarterfinals. ● All four singles finalists are Czechoslovakian-born, with Martina Navratilova defeating Helena Sukova, 6-3, 6-2, for the women's title, and Ivan Lendl besting Miloslav Mecir, 6-4, 6-2, 6-0, for the men's crown.

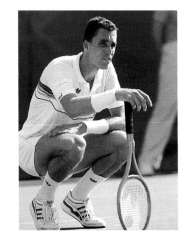

1987 Michael Chang, at the age of 15 years, six mo and 10 days, becomes the youngest man to win a match the US Open, defeating Paul McNamee in the first round. Chris Evert's streak of 16 straight US Open semifinal appe ances is ended by Lori McNeil in the quarterfinals. ● On 100th anniversary of the first women's championships, Ma Navratilova wins the Triple Crown, defeating Steffi Graf, 7-6 6-1, for the singles title, teaming with Pam Shriver to win t women's doubles and pairing with Emilio Sanchez to win mixed doubles. ● Ivan Lendl (left) wins his third straight defeating Mats Wilander, 6-7, 6-0, 7-6, 6-4, in a four-hour, 47-minute men's final played on Monday due to rain.

A FOND FAREWELL

Chris Evert had, in essence, opened her career at the US Open, so it seemed fitting she would end it there as well. In 1989, she announced that the US Open—her 19th consecutive one—would be her last.

No one figured that Evert's quarterfinal match against Zina Garrison would be the last match of her final US Open, especially after she had played so brilliantly in the previous round, knocking off 15-year-old Monica Seles. Against Garrison, Evert opened up with a 5-2 first-set lead but saw it slip away into a 7-6 loss. Garrison won the second set easily, 6-2, as a career and an era simultaneously came to an end. Evert gathered her racquets, gave a last wave to the crowd, and disappeared into the Stadium tunnel. ●

1988 Seventeen-year-old Pete Sampras makes his US Open debut, losing in the first round to Jaime Yzaga, 6-7, 6-7, 6-4, 7-5, 6-2. ● A stomach flu nearly wipes out a full day's schedule on Stadium Court as Chris Evert and Rick Leach are forced to default their respective women's singles semifinal and men's doubles final matches. ● Steffi Graf becomes the third woman to complete the Grand Slam, defeating Gabriela Sabatini in the final, 6-3, 3-6, 6-1. Graf goes on to win the gold medal in women's singles at the Olympics in Seoul, Korea, giving her a "Golden Slam." ● Mats Wilander (left) outlasts Ivan Lendl, 6-4, 4-6, 6-3, 5-7, 6-4, in four hours and 55 minutes—the longest men's final in US Open history—and wrests the world's No. 1 ranking from Lendl.

1989 Chris Evert, playing in her last US Open, defeats 15-year-old Monica Seles for her 101st and final US Open singles victory before losing to Zina Garrison (right) in the quarterfinals, 7-6, 6-2. ● Trailing by a set and a service break, Steffi Graf comes back to defeat Martina Navratilova in the women's final, 3-6, 7-5, 6-1. ● Boris Becker makes it a German sweep of the singles titles, defeating Ivan Lendl in the men's final, 7-6, 1-6, 6-3, 7-6.

Clockwise from top left: Ivan Lendl, 1985. *Melchior DiGiacomo;* Arthur Ashe, 1975. *Melchior DiGiacomo;* John McEnroe, 1979. *Carrie Boretz;* Jimmy Connors, 1980. *Carrie Boretz*

Serena Williams, 2007. *Elsa/Getty Images*

Jimmy Connors, 1982. *AP Images/Ron Frehm*

DID AN ERA END AT THE 1981 US OPEN?

by Peter Bodo

Bjorn Borg reached the US Open men's singles final four times in a six-year span but failed to take home the trophy each time, losing first to Jimmy Connors (1976 and 1978) and then to John McEnroe (1980 and 1981). Following that last defeat, Peter Bodo in the November 1981 issue of TENNIS *speculated—correctly, as it turned out—that McEnroe's victory over Borg at the 1981 US Open might signal a major change at the top of the pro game.*

THE CLOCK SAID 6:32 P.M., and the scoreboard high above the stadium court at Flushing Meadow showed that Wimbledon champion John McEnroe led Wimbledon legend Bjorn Borg by two sets to one and 3-2 in the men's singles final of the 1981 US Open. For once, there was no jet thundering through the New York haze. The only sunlight left was a lavish orange smear on the windows of the press box high in the stadium. The finalists had just exchanged service breaks and Borg stood at 30-all, two points from evening up the set. In the serene light, the full stadium resembled a bowl lavishly filled with wildflowers.

Borg prepared to deliver a second serve. As usual, his long hair and headband hid his face, a face that had stared into a similar abyss numerous times. Tossing the ball, coming out of his crouch to reach into his fate, Borg placed the serve to McEnroe's backhand. The return floated back so softly you could almost hear the ball purring. Borg took the ball on the backhand slide and drove it long. It was 30-40. A whisper of surprise, perhaps consternation, passed through the crowd.

Once again, Borg missed his first serve. Once again, he served the second ball to McEnroe's backhand and again the return was neutral, an invitation rather than an act of aggression. Then, for one of the few times in his distinguished career as a player of consummate desire and unassailable nerve, Borg turned down the invitation. Once again, the two-fisted backhand, which had been favorably compared to the hammer of Thor, sent the ball beyond the baseline. Game. McEnroe.

There would be no more service breaks, and McEnroe would beat Borg, 4-6, 6-2, 6-4, 6-3, becoming the first man to win three consecutive U.S. Championships since Bill Tilden had done it en route to six straight titles more than a half-century ago. Later, when the pundits discussed the turning points, key games and strategic matters, that particular game would not figure in the conversations. Yet the image from that still, secret moment remains: the placid champion serving into the twilight and on two nearly identical occasions failing not only to win the important points but failing even to set them in motion.

Chris Evert Lloyd has said that there comes a time in the lives of all great players when the nerves suddenly and unexpectedly rebel, when they will no longer respond to the pressure with superhuman authority. Careers sometimes hinge on such occasions. We remember the 1977 Wimbledon final, in which Jimmy Connors snarled back from an 0-4 deficit in the fifth set to pull even with Borg, only to serve a crucial double fault that swung the match back in Borg's favor. With that match, the flicker crept into the flame that is Connors.

Now, Borg may be in the same position. He will undoubtedly continue to win big titles, just as Connors did after handing the keys to Wimbledon over to the Swede. Yet the aura has evaporated.

Just two years ago, Borg explained that he played the important points so well because when they came along, he grew relaxed and felt he had nothing to lose. After the Swede once again dispelled the spectre of Roscoe Tanner at this year's Open, he said something different. "Even for me," Borg confessed, "it is sometimes difficult to relax during some big points." His audience laughed. Borg looked surprised; then he smiled to himself.

McEnroe put it this way after the final: "I thought Bjorn got careless after the first set, and then it didn't seem like he was sure what he wanted to do. I've always said it's a lot tougher to stay at the top than to get there,

Bjorn Borg and John McEnroe, 1981. *Fred Mullane/Camerawork USA*

Bjorn Borg's broken racquet, 1981. *Carrie Boretz*

so I can't really understand why Bjorn keeps saying that he wants this title so much. It should be obvious to everybody that he does, especially because I won at Wimbledon. He just puts himself under incredible pressure, and you have to figure that after a while the pressure gets to everybody." Even Borg.

———

Just as he had at Wimbledon in July, John McEnroe played his best, his only truly focused match, on the final day. Through the pre-liminary rounds, he was a lethargic competitor, casually destroying small creatures while he awaited the arrival of the Big Game.

McEnroe dropped a set to Juan Nunez on the opening day and, in the quarterfinals, he was almost ambushed by India's young Ramesh Krishnan. Krishnan won the first set and served for the second, only to put the vital 30-all point into the net with an aborted drop shot. With typical candor, McEnroe later confessed, "You never want to take a guy lightly, but sometimes you do."

If anything, Borg had the opposite problem. Once again, he seemed tight and tentative against routine opponents. One of his more troublesome antagonists, Yannick Noah, framed the imminent Borg-McEnroe final in an accurate perspective. After losing to Borg in four sets, Noah said, "It seems to me that Borg was playing better last year. Maybe there is less pressure on him now that he doesn't have to worry about the Grand Slam and maybe he feels he needs this title badly. But McEnroe wants it badly, too. Borg may be angry because he lost at Wimbledon, but McEnroe knows that if they play, it is for number one in the world."

Ultimately, the decisive factor in the final was not the state of Borg's serve but his state of mind and McEnroe's multifaceted game. After Borg took he first set, McEnroe took control and, just as at Wimbledon, he would not relinquish it.

Unexpectedly, McEnroe's finest game was one of defense, not offense. Down a break at 3-4 in the third, McEnroe broke back with four superb winners. Two of them were crosscourt backhand passing shots of paralyzing velocity. The other two were topspin lobs. Each of them left Borg rooted at the net as they fell like flakes of snow for winners. And when Borg does not even make a serious move to run down a lob, we know that a perfect shot has been struck.

John McEnroe, 1981. *Stephen Szurlej/TENNIS*

"I used the topspin lob a lot in the past," McEnroe said after it was all over. "Then, I let it fall out of my game. I guess it's time to bring it back."

While McEnroe spoke, Borg, the subject of death threats on each of the last two days of the tournament, was sequestered in the locker room. Although he did not know of the threats until after his matches, they might have been a factor. The press never found out, because a host of security men whisked the Swede out through a back entrance. The grim finalist was last seen behind the wheel of a white Saab 900 Turbo, driving with his omnipresent coach, Lennart Bergelin, into the New York night.

Lindsay Davenport, 2006. *Nick Laham/Getty Images*

South Plaza from Arthur Ashe Stadium, 2007. *Getty Images*

THE GOLDEN AGE

by Steve Flink

In 1988, Steffi Graf became the first player to complete the Grand Slam on the hard courts of Flushing Meadows. Steve Flink recalled in the 1998 edition of the US Open tournament magazine how the 19-year-old Graf made history with a remarkable campaign that she capped off by winning the gold medal at the Summer Olympics in Seoul, making her the first to achieve the "Golden Slam."

CAPTURING THE GRAND SLAM, sweeping the four major championships in a single season, is perhaps the most elusive goal of all for the great players. Sixty years ago, J. Donald Budge became the first champion to realize that remarkable feat. Maureen "Little Mo" Connolly was the next to pull it off, in 1953. Following the successes of those two immensely gifted Americans, a pair of Australians joined the exclusive Grand Slam club. Rod Laver did it twice, in 1962 and 1969, and Margaret Court made it her career milestone in 1970. All those Grand Slams were completed at Forest Hills on the fabled grass courts of the West Side Tennis Club. But the fifth and last player to gain this arduous accomplishment finished her business here on the hard courts at Flushing Meadows, and she was none other than Steffi Graf.

This is the 10th anniversary of Graf's strikingly smooth passage through the major championships of 1988. The German turned 19 in the middle of that year, and her timing and temerity could hardly have been better. Graf had taken over the No. 1 world ranking the previous year when she had secured her first Grand Slam tournament title at Roland Garros in Paris. Despite subsequent losses to an enduring Martina Navratilova in the 1987 finals of Wimbledon and the US Open, it was very apparent as the 1988 season began that Graf was going to be the dominant force in her sport. Both Navratilova and Chris Evert—the two prodigious champions who had controlled the women's game between them since the mid-1970s—were fading slightly, and none of the younger brigade of ascending competitors could quite keep up with Graf.

The fact remains that no one was fully prepared for Graf's unwavering pride, power and professionalism over the course of that season. Few observers anticipated her capacity to build on one triumph after another without breaking down. Hardly anyone believed Graf, at that springtime stretch in her career, would demonstrate such consistency and conviction

every time it counted. To be sure, not even Graf had any strong notions about taking such a monumental historical leap.

And yet, Graf simply took her journey through the majors one match and one event at a time, never looking too far ahead, refusing to dwell on the triumphs she had left behind her.

Her campaign commenced at the new Flinders Park facility in Melbourne, featuring a modern stadium court with a retractable roof, the first of its kind. The final, against Chris Evert, began outdoors, with the German leading 2-1 in the opening set. The competitors were then forced off court for 89 minutes by rain, and when they returned, the roof was put in operation. Graf adjusted much more easily to the indoor conditions, and she closed out the contest, 6-1, 7-6 (3). Steffi was on her way.

Next stop, Roland Garros. Having conquered the field on the Rebound Ace hard courts in Melbourne, Graf shifted to the slow red-clay courts in Paris and was every bit as determined and dynamic. As was the case in Australia, Graf swept all seven of her matches emphatically in straight sets. In the final, Graf obliterated Natasha Zvereva, 6-0, 6-0, in 32 minutes.

On to Wimbledon, where Graf reached the final without even coming close to the loss of a set, extending her streak to 40 consecutive sets and 20 Grand Slam matches in a row. Waiting for her in the championship match was the redoubtable Martina Navratilova, who exploited her superb grass-court skills to build a 7-5, 2-0 lead. But Steffi proceeded to stage a sweeping reversal of fortune and collected 12 of the last 13 games in a 5-7, 6-2, 6-1 victory.

As Steffi approached her last and most demanding assignment, on the hard courts of New York, Margaret Court said, "More than anything, winning the Grand Slam is a battle within yourself. It really gets down to how you handle pressure more than how you handle anybody else. Steffi has to forget about the press and the television and not read and listen to what people say about her. You don't want to let the pressure build within yourself."

Ann Haydon Jones, the astute British left-hander who toppled Court and Billie Jean King to win Wimbledon in 1969, liked Graf's chances of

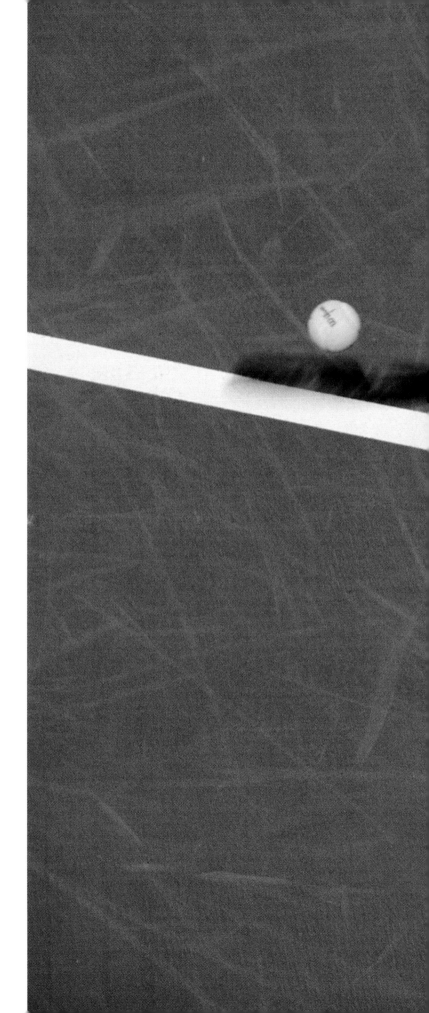

securing the Slam. As Jones pointed out, "Steffi's chances of winning the Slam are very good, about 90 percent I would think, as long as she stays healthy. Margaret was a great athlete with all the strokes, but to me Steffi has stronger nerves than Margaret. And Steffi has proven she can win on every surface, which can only add to her confidence."

Both Court and Jones were very much on the mark. Graf chalked up five consecutive straight-set victories and was slated to meet Evert in the penultimate round. But Chris had come down with food poisoning and was in no condition to compete. For the only time in her 56-tournament Grand Slam career, Evert defaulted, and Graf was through to the final. By now she had posted 26 straight "Big Four" match victories with the loss of only one set, and only one woman stood between Steffi and the Grand Slam.

Gabriela Sabatini fully believed she could beat Graf in the US Open final, and her heavy doses of topspin did disrupt Graf in the middle of the final. But, in the end, Graf was too potent off the forehand and too resourceful in pulling away for a 6-3, 3-6, 6-1 win. She had lost a trace of her efficiency in the second set, but with the whole season on the line in the third set, her execution was supreme.

In the post-match ceremony, Don Budge stood alongside Graf to celebrate the honor they shared, and Budge told the teenager that he thought she could win another Grand Slam in the years ahead. He was very nearly correct in that projection. The following year, in 1989, Graf won three of the four majors, losing only the French Open final to Arantxa Sanchez Vicario. But she had a 5-3 final-set lead in that confrontation. Three times thereafter, Graf has had the same level of success. She won three of the four Grand Slam events again in 1993, 1995 and 1996. On the latter two occasions, she was unable to play the Australian Open as injuries kept her away from the action.

But, in 1988, Graf established herself as only the third woman and fifth player to win all four majors in a single year. And then she achieved something no Slammer had ever done, taking the gold medal at the Olympic Games in Seoul, South Korea, defeating Sabatini again in the final round. With that additional triumph of significance, Graf had recorded the first "Golden Slam." She would win 72 of 75 matches across that season, and 11 of 14 tournaments. Following up on that sterling year, she collected 16 more major titles from 1989–96 to lift her career total to 21 Grand Slam singles tournament crowns.

She has had an astonishingly long run at, and near, the top of the game. But she's never had another year quite like 1988.

Jennifer Capriati, 2003. *AP Images/Amy Sancetta*

Monica Seles, 1997. *AP Images/Bill Koustron*

Andre Agassi and Pete Sampras, 1990. *Stephen Szurlej/TENNIS*

A GALAXY OF STARS

The Gen-X decade brought with it a new era of communication, as the World Wide Web sprang to life in 1992. Prior to that, Spam was just meat in a can. Before the Web had gone up, the Wall had come down, and the reuniting of East and West Berlin made Americans feel especially warm in the realization that the Cold War had ended. America's president was popular with many, and too popular with some. It seemed like everyone had a talk show or a reality show—though hardly any of it could ever pass as real. O.J. ran but got caught; politicians got caught, but kept running. It turned out that life is like a box of chocolates—you never know what you're going to get.

The US Open during this decade was likewise full of surprises. It began with back-to-back years in which Pete Sampras, at 19, became the US Open's youngest-ever men's champion and Jimmy Connors, at 39, made an unforgettable charge to the semis. It ended with a brilliant win by an equally luminous young star—Serena Williams—who became the first African-American woman in more than four decades to claim the US Open women's crown. In between all of that, the US Open was twice captured by a reluctant Swede, Stefan Edberg, and twice more by a rebellious American, Andre Agassi. All told, Sampras won four times in the 1990s, Steffi Graf was three times a champion and Monica Seles triumphed twice.

But there were also visits to the winner's circle by Gabriela Sabatini, Arantxa Sanchez-Vicario and Patrick Rafter—twice. Cedric Pioline, Greg Rusedski and Mark Philippoussis (who, perhaps fittingly, would later have his own reality show) all reached the final. That variety of champions and finalists translated into a variety of classic matches, as the game's biggest names collided furiously on New York's hard acres.

As the game's best got better, so did the US Open. In 1997, the tournament opened the magnificent Arthur Ashe Stadium, providing a fittingly grand stage for an ever-growing galaxy of enormous stars.

the CHAMPIONS

	MEN'S SINGLES	WOMEN'S SINGLES
1990	Pete Sampras	Gabriela Sabatini
1991	Stefan Edberg	Monica Seles
1992	Stefan Edberg	Monica Seles
1993	Pete Sampras	Steffi Graf
1994	Andre Agassi	Arantxa Sanchez-Vicario
1995	Pete Sampras	Steffi Graf
1996	Pete Sampras	Steffi Graf
1997	Patrick Rafter	Martina Hingis
1998	Patrick Rafter	Lindsay Davenport
1999	Andre Agassi	Serena Williams

Points in Time

1992 MEN'S SEMIFINALS

Stefan Edberg d. Michael Chang, 6-7, 7-5, 7-6, 5-7, 6-4 Stefan Edberg (left) outlasted Michael Chang in the longest recorded match in US Open history, five hours and 26 minutes. It was the last of three consecutive matches in which Edberg rallied from a break-down in the fifth set to win, having also done so in the fourth round against Richard Krajicek and in the quarterfinals against Ivan Lendl. Edberg went on to defeat Pete Sampras in four sets in a final that pitted the last two men's singles champions, Sampras in 1990 and Edberg in 1991. ●

1996 MEN'S QUARTERFINALS

Pete Sampras d. Alex Corretja, 7-6, 5-7, 5-7, 6-4, 7-6

No. 31 Alex Corretja figured as little more than a distraction for defending champion Pete Sampras (left). Yet the Spaniard put up a magnificent battle, and as the match played on, neither man wanted to be the first to yield—either to his opponent or to exhaustion. In the fifth-set tie-break, Sampras, dehydrated and wobbly, began vomiting and was given a warning for taking too much time between points. At 6-7 in the tie-break, Sampras fought off match point with a lunging forehand volley. At 7-all, Sampras missed wildly on a first serve, then whipped in a second-serve ace. Stunned, Corretja double-faulted, and the match was over. ●

1995 WOMEN'S FINAL

Steffi Graf d. Monica Seles, 7-6, 0-6, 6-3

More than two years after a brutal stabbing derailed Monica Seles's career, she was back in the US Open final against Steffi Graf, her longtime rival. Graf and Seles were seeded No. 1 and No. 2, respectively, and at least one of them had appeared in the US Open final each year since 1987. This marked the first time they met for the title, however, and the match lived up to its billing. Graf won the first-set tie-break, 8-6. Down a set, Seles ran down every ball and hit winner after winner to dominate the second set and even the match. In the final set, Graf changed her game plan. Aware that Seles had yet to play so hard and long in her comeback, Graf took a bit off her shots and tried to make the points last a little longer. She jumped out to a lead and held on in what she would later call her greatest victory. ●

the HIGHLIGHTS

1990 Stefan Edberg is dismissed in straight sets by Alexander Volkov and becomes only the second No. 1 seed in the Open era to lose in the first round. ● Fourteen-year-old Jennifer Capriati (left) makes her US Open debut, advancing to the fourth round before falling to Steffi Graf. ● Gabriela Sabatini upsets Steffi Graf in the women's final, 6-2, 7-6, to win her lone Grand Slam singles title. ● Pete Sampras, at the age of 19 years and 28 days, becomes the youngest US Open men's singles champion, defeating Andre Agassi in the men's final, 6-4, 6-3, 6-2. The 12th-seeded Sampras is also the lowest men's seed to win the US Open. ●

FAN-FARE

What makes the US Open unique, what sets it apart from its Grand Slam partners, is that it's less about court characteristics than it is about characters. Ask any player for his or her take on playing at the US Open, and the answer will invariably wind its way toward a discourse on the fans who populate the Flushing Meadows fortnight. The hard courts may not play favorites, but the fans more than make up for the surface's unfailing neutrality.

Perhaps it's because the US Open is accessible to the average fan. Or maybe it's the fan-friendly layout of the US Open grounds. Or simply that it's New York, where so many are so willing to share so many opinions. Whatever the reasons, the US Open in the 1990s truly blossomed as the Fans' Slam. And that special relationship between the US Open and its fans has continued to flower every year.

1991 A fifteen-year-old Lindsay Davenport makes her US Open debut, losing in the first round to Debbie Graham. ● Wild-card-entrant Jimmy Connors makes a stunning run to the semifinals. Ranked No. 174, he rallies from 4-6, 6-7, 0-3, 0-40 to defeat Patrick McEnroe in a first-round match that ends at 1:35 a.m. And on his 39th birthday, Connor comes back from a two-sets-to-one and a 2-5 fifth-set deficit to outlast Aaron Krickstein in the fourth round. ● Monica Seles defeats Martina Navratilova, 7-6, 6-1, in the women's final for her first US Open title. ● Stefan Edberg becomes the first player to win the US Open one year after losing in the first round by dismissing Jim Courier (left) in the men's final, 6-3, 6-3, 6-2.

1992 In his record 115th and final US Open singles match, Jimmy Connors is defeated in a second-round night match by Ivan Lendl, 3-6, 6-3, 6-2, 6-0. ● John McEnroe tops Richard Fromberg in a third-round match in what is ultimately McEnroe's final US Open singles victory. ● Players from the U.S. sweep all four junior championships, with Lindsay Davenport winning the girls' singles and doubles (with Nicole London), Brian Dunn capturing the boys' singles and J.J. Jackson and Eric Taino teaming up for the boys' doubles. ● Monica Seles repeats as US Open champion by defeating Arantxa Sanchez-Vicario in the women's final, 6-3, 6-3. ● Stefan Edberg (left) wins three straight five-set matches to reach the men's singles final, where he dispatches Pete Sampras, 3-6, 6-4, 7-6, 6-2.

ARTHUR ASHE KIDS' DAY

A showcase for promoting and increasing interest in tennis, Arthur Ashe Kids' Day annually kicks off the US Open by bringing together the sports and entertainment worlds for a full-day tennis and music festival for children and families. The day includes interactive games, free tennis clinics and a show that features the biggest names in tennis—including Andre Agassi, John McEnroe, Martina Navratilova and Venus and Serena Williams—and some of the hottest acts in music. In fact, over the years Arthur Ashe Kids' Day has become renowned for its musical performers, such as the Backstreet Boys, the Jonas Brothers, Vanessa Carlton, the Cheetah Girls, Jesse McCartney, 98 Degrees, Rihanna, Britney Spears and Jessica Simpson.

The inaugural Arthur Ashe Kids' Day was held at the start of the 1996 US Open, merging two previous existing events—the Arthur Ashe AIDS Tennis Challenge and Kids' Day—and proving an unqualified success. In the years that have followed, the day has continued to honor tennis legend Arthur Ashe and carry on his mission of using tennis as a means to instill in kids the values of humanitarianism, leadership and academic excellence, with the event benefiting a variety of youth-oriented charities and USTA NJTL (National Junior Tennis League). ●

the HIGHLIGHTS

1993 Grounds passes are sold for the first time. ● Goran Ivanisevic and Daniel Nestor play the longest tie-break in US Open history: 38 points, with Ivanisevic prevailing, 20-18, in the third and final set. ● Mats Wilander defeats Mikael Pernfors, in a four-hour-and-one-minute five-setter that ends at 2:26 a.m.—the latest conclusion ever of a US Open match. ● Steffi Graf wins her third US Open title with a 6-3, 6-3 victory over Helena Sukova in the women's final. ● No. 2 seed Pete Sampras collects his second US Open title by defeating Cedric Pioline in the men's final, 6-4, 6-4, 6-3.

US Open Trophies

Since the advent of Open tennis, the USTA has awarded perpetual silver championship trophies to the winners during an on-court ceremony at the conclusion of the final-round matches. The trophies are then sent to international fine jeweler and silversmith Tiffany & Co. to be engraved with the names of the new champions before being returned to their year-round home at the International Tennis Hall of Fame in Newport, Rhode Island. Each US Open champion receives a replica trophy engraved with their name to commemorate the achievement.

The men's singles trophy stands 19.5 inches high, 16 inches wide (handle to handle), is seven inches in diameter and weighs seven pounds. The women's singles trophy is slightly smaller than the men's, standing 12 inches high, 14.5 inches wide (handle to handle). It is seven inches in diameter and weighs five pounds. The replica trophies sent to both the men's and women's singles champions are the size of the men's singles perpetual trophy. Bowls are awarded to the winners of the men's doubles, women's doubles and mixed doubles competitions.

One of a Kind Saddled with the label of "underachiever" at the relatively young age of 24, Andre Agassi arrived at the 1994 US Open unseeded and searching to regain the form that made him a US Open finalist just four years earlier.

The result was one of the more surprising title runs of the Open era. Agassi knocked off a record five seeded players, including fellow Americans Michael Chang and Todd Martin, to win his second career Grand Slam men's singles title and his first US Open championship. By defeating No. 4 seed Michael Stich, 6-1, 7-6, 7-5, in the final, Agassi became the first unseeded player in the Open era to win a US Open singles crown and the first overall since Fred Stolle defeated John Newcombe in 1966.

The championship was a stunning development for a player who had dropped to No. 32 in the world earlier in the year and had not advanced past the quarterfinals of a Grand Slam event since winning Wimbledon in 1992. But it would presage great things to come. Agassi added a second title at the end of the decade, defeating Martin in a five-set final in 1999, and appeared in six US Open finals in his career—the last one against Roger Federer in 2005. Agassi retired the following year, having played in 21 consecutive US Opens, an Open era record.

1994 Ivan Lendl plays what becomes his final professional tennis match when he is forced to retire with back pain against Bernd Karbacher in the second round. ● Arantxa Sanchez-Vicario (left) defeats Steffi Graf in the women's singles final, 1-6, 7-6, 6-4, and teams with Jana Novotna to win the women's doubles. ● Andre Agassi enters the tournament ranked No. 20 and knocks off a record five seeded players—including No. 4 seed Michael Stich, 6-1, 7-6, 7-5, in the men's final—to become the first unseeded player in the Open era to win the US Open.

1995 For the first time ever at the US Open, four players who have all been ranked No. 1 in the world reach the men's semifinals, with Andre Agassi defeating Boris Becker and Pete Sampras topping Jim Courier. ● Despite losing the second set 6-0, Steffi Graf wins her fourth US Open singles crown with a 7-6, 0-6, 6-3 victory over Monica Seles in the women's final. ● No. 2 seed Pete Sampras wins his third US Open men's singles title, defeating top-seeded Andre Agassi, 6-4, 6-3, 4-6, 7-5, in the final.

Parade of Champions

It's never easy planning a party. But on the night of August 25, 1997, the proceedings couldn't have been more perfect. Every living U.S. singles champion was invited to take part in the dedication of Arthur Ashe Stadium, the USTA National Tennis Center's sparkling new centerpiece, named for the late champion and humanitarian. There were nearly as many stars on court as in the night sky, which exploded with fireworks as pop diva Whitney Houston serenaded the assembled throng.

The building of Arthur Ashe Stadium was part of a $285 million expansion and enhancement, which included the renovation of Louis Armstrong Stadium and a facelift of the grounds of the USTA National Tennis Center, the world's largest public tennis facility and home of the US Open.

The site now allows nearly 40,000 fans to watch the greatest tennis in the world during each session of the US Open. That's almost three times as many fans who attended the largest session of the 1968 US Open, which Arthur Ashe won at the West Side Tennis Club in Forest Hills.

the HIGHLIGHTS

1996 Defending champion and No. 1 seed Pete Sampras, fighting off fatigue and becoming ill on court, outlasts Alex Corretja in the quarterfinals, 7-6, 5-7, 5-7, 6-4, 6-7, in one of the most dramatic US Open matches ever. ● The last US Open singles championship matches are played in Louis Armstrong Stadium. ● Steffi Graf does not lose a set all tournament as she wins her fifth and final US Open women's singles title, defeating Monica Seles, 7-5, 6-4, for the championship. ● With the No. 1 ranking at stake, top-seeded Pete Sampras subdues No. 2 seed Michael Chang (left) in the men's final, 6-1, 6-4, 7-6, for his fourth US Open singles crown. It is Sampras' first Grand Slam tournament title since the death of his close friend and coach, Tim Gullikson, who would have celebrated his 45th birthday on the day of the men's final.

1997 The US Open becomes a coming-out party, as Arthur Ashe Stadium opens as the centerpiece of an expanded and enhanced USTA National Tennis Center. ● Venus Williams and Irina Spirlea duke it out in one of the mo dramatic women's semifinal matches in US Open history, wi Williams prevailing, 7-6, 4-6, 7-6, after overcoming two matc points and a controversial changeover collision with Spirlea. ● Sixteen-year-old Martina Hingis and 17-year-old Venus Williams play the youngest Grand Slam women's final in the Open era, with Hingis winning, 6-0, 6-4. ● Patrick Rafter outduels Greg Rusedski in the men's final, 6-3, 6-2, 4-6, 7-5

1998 Patrick Rafter saves himself from the dubious distinction of becoming the first US Open defending champion to lose in the first round by coming back from two-sets-to-love to defeat Hicham Arazi. ● Patty Schnyder defeats Steffi Graf in the round of 16 in what ultimately becomes Graf's final match at the US Open. ● Lindsay Davenport wins her first Grand Slam singles title, defeating Martina Hingis, 6-3, 7-5, in the women's final. ● Patrick Rafter (left) repeats as US Open singles champion, defeating Mark Philippoussis, 6-3, 3-6, 6-2, 6-0, for the men's title.

1999 The rededication of Louis Armstrong Stadium marks the completion of the USTA National Tennis Center's $285-million expansion project, which spanned the terms of six USTA presidents. ● Patrick Rafter becomes the first defending US Open champion to lose in the first round, retiring in the fourth set against Cedric Pioline due to a shoulder injury. ● Todd Martin stages another in a series of great comebacks at the US Open, defeating Greg Rusedski, who served for the match at 5-4 in the third set and led 4-1 in the fifth. Martin wins 20 of the final 21 points to advance into the quarterfinals. ● Richard Krajicek serves a record 49 aces in his quarterfinal loss to Yevgeny Kafelnikov. ● Serena Williams (right), seeded No. 7, defeats top-seeded Martina Hingis in the women's final, 6-3, 7-6. ● Andre Agassi never loses his serve in defeating Todd Martin in the men's final, 6-4, 6-7, 6-7, 6-3, 6-2.

The Grandstand, 2003. *Getty Images*

Clockwise from top left: Hana Mandlikova, 1982. *Carrie Boretz;* Ivan Lendl, 1983. *Carrie Boretz;* Boris Becker, 1990. *Melchior DiGiacomo;* Martina Navartilova, 1983. *Carrie Boretz*

Martina Hingis, 1997. *AP Images/Hans Deryk*

CONNORS STEALS THE SHOW

by Norm Zeitchick

Jimmy Connors, 39 years old and ranked No. 174, put an indelible stamp on the 1991 US Open by making a run to the semifinals that was as entertaining as it was remarkable. Norm Zeitchick watched the drama unfold and recounted in the November 1991 issue of TENNIS *Connors's unrelenting drive to remain No. 1 in the hearts of the fans.*

IN THE END, it was Monica Seles's ferocious ground attack and Stefan Edberg's flawless serve and volley that prevailed. But for two weeks it was the electricity of 39-year-old Jimmy Connors, the Lazarus of tennis, that lit up the US Open and taught us what the sport is all about.

Both first-time winners Seles and Edberg also vaulted back into the No. 1 spots on their respective tours. Seles reigned atop the rankings most of the year, but in late summer she and Steffi Graf seesawed at that position, as Edberg and Boris Becker had done throughout the year.

Seles survived a three-set slugfest in the semifinals with the youngest player in the women's draw, 15-year-old Jennifer Capriati, then in the final she dismantled the relentless attack of the oldest player, Martina Navratilova, 7-6, 6-1. Her first US Open crown gave Seles three of this year's four Grand Slam titles. She withdrew from Wimbledon amid a storm of controversy.

"It feels great," said a bubbly Seles afterward. "Probably the happiest whenever I won a Grand Slam."

Edberg beat another first-time finalist, Jim Courier, 6-2, 6-4, 6-0. Courier hadn't dropped a set and had derailed the Connors express in the semifinals before running into the high-bounding serves and surgical volleys of the Swede. "This is probably the best match I ever played," Edberg fairly gushed after his triumph. "I'm even beginning to like New York, too."

One player who definitely loves New York is Connors, who defied age (39), ranking (No. 174) and seeding (he received a wild card into the draw) to give the performance of a lifetime. It almost didn't happen. Playing a first-round night match against Patrick McEnroe, Connors was down two sets and 0-3 in the third. It was past midnight, and most of the faithful had gone home or turned off their TV sets. But the competitive spark that has smoldered in the five-time Open champion for 20 years erupted that night into a supernova that kept the entire tournament starstruck.

It's not just his age, though it's remarkable that he still can play at such a high level. It's not just his will to win, though nobody has ever come back from the brink as often or as dramatically as he has. It's that Connors puts everything—body and soul—into his game, with a joyous, competitive zeal that's contagious.

"Every time I play now, it's a final," mused Connors. "I never, ever thought I'd play tennis again [after surgery for a wrist injury]. And because of that, my enthusiasm and my intensity and my enjoyment of the game is all lifted to . . . somewhere else. To have those cheers ringing down like that, that is what you break your back for *every* time you walk out there."

In so doing, he intimately involves every member of the audience in his struggle. They feel the exhilaration of the attack, the thrill of the putaway or impossible get. And the energy of the crowd pumps Connors to play beyond what he alone could accomplish. The synergy between audience and performance

Jimmy Connors, 1991. *Stephen Szurlej/TENNIS*

elevates a Connors match beyond sport; it's a symphony in short pants, an epiphany of sweat.

Pat Mac heard the music first hand that night. As Connors clawed and scratched back into the match, the vocal few that remained in the stadium carried Jimbo to a five-set triumph that ended at 1:35 in the morning.

"There's a pattern that has been set throughout my career—you're going to have to kill me to beat me," Connors said afterward. "I'm going to do what it takes to win until the last minute. It's what I do best." Just ask Michael Schapers and 10th-seeded Karel Novacek, who succumbed in straight sets as Connors stormed into the round of 16.

There, before an overflow crowd on his birthday, Connors played the match of the tournament against Aaron Krickstein, who had knocked out eighth-seeded Andre Agassi in the first round. (Not surprisingly, nobody missed tennis's poster boy, unless you count Nike, which had no one to preen in the new outfits it had created for him)

Connors was down one set and 1-5 in the second, when for old time's sake an airplane roared over the stadium. Rumor had it that New York City mayor David Dinkins, present in a ring-side seat, had ordered the distraction to help out his old buddy. Connors obligingly roared back to win the set in a tie-break, incited by the crowd and a volatile, overrule protest. Nursing a sore knee, he fell behind in the third set, won the fourth, only to find himself on the brink of extinction, down 2-5 in the fifth. Krickstein is a marathoner who'd never lost a five-setter at the Open, but he never faced such a relentless charge, as Connors stared down defeat. Twenty thousand people held their breath as Jimbo attacked the net at every opportunity, forced a fifth-set tie-break, then willed himself to victory.

"I don't mind opening up my chest and showing my heart," said Connors. "That's what tennis is all about."

Heart was definitely the issue for defending champion Pete Sampras, who seemed almost relieved after being blown out by

Jimmy Connors fans, 1991. *Stephen Szurlej/TENNIS*

an impressive Courier in the quarters. "It is tough to come to a match being the defending champion," he said in defeat. "It is kind of like the monkey is off my back."

That kind of talk astounds an old battle-ax like Connors. "I spent my whole life trying to win seven of these," he reflected. "That is the greatest feeling you could have, to be the US Open champion. If these guys aren't living for that, then something is wrong."

To emphasize his point, Connors reached inside himself again in the quarters to beat Paul Haarhuis, who had knocked a wounded Becker out of the tournament in the third round. Overcoming a sluggish start, Connors turned the match around on a single point that belied belief. Scrambling to return four overheads in succession, Connors finally won the point with a running backhand down the line to break both Haarhuis's serve and spirit. It was the crowning jewel in a sparkling performance.

As Connors thrived, others struggled to survive the 90-degree temperatures, the distractions and the heated competition that makes the Open such a pressure-cooker. . . . Connors's influence reached even into the women's draw, which lay dormant until the quarterfinals. "He's an inspiration," said the sixth-seeded, 34-year-old Navratilova. "If he can do it at that age, so can I. I'm a spring chicken compared to him." Finally finding her serve again, Navratilova attacked with reckless abandon, winning consecutive three-set, two-tie-break thrillers over Arantxa Sanchez-Vicario and No. 1 Steffi Graf to get to the final.

So the Open has two new champions, but the buzz from the oldest is ringing still. Tellingly, during one press conference, "I Am No Longer The Reigning Open Champion" Sampras complained, "Is this about Connors or about me?"

Silly question, Pete. ●

Court coverage., 2006. *Getty Images*

Bjorn Borg, 1975. *Steve Szurlej/TENNIS*

Monica Seles, 2002. *Getty Images*

Grandstand View, 2007. *USTA*

121

int

Guillermo Vilas, 1977. *AP Images/Suzanne Vlamis*

Pete Sampras, 1992. *Fred Mullane/Camerawork USA*

PLAYING IT CLOSE TO THE NET

by Doug Smith

As the 1994 US Open was about to begin, Pete Sampras, the defending champion, was still far removed from realizing his ultimate totals of eight US Open finals and five US Open crowns. But his greatness was already very much in evidence, and in the 1994 US Open tournament magazine Doug Smith took a close look at "a legend-in-the-making."

PETE SAMPRAS, ARMED mainly with a sizzling serve, bolted into the upper echelons of pro tennis at the 1990 US Open. This year, the laid-back, boy-next-door Californian, now residing in Tampa, Florida, goes for US Open title No. III.

Sampras, then just 19, became the youngest male to claim the prestigious Grand Slam title, defeating—in succession—Ivan Lendl, John McEnroe and Andre Agassi in the final three rounds. In seven US Open matches, Sampras, whose first serve frequently was clocked at 120 mph, fired 100 aces. His power-packed serve prompted some to nickname him "Pistol Pete."

But after capturing his second US Open title in 1993, Sampras solidified himself as a legend-in-the-making and made two points quite clear: (1) He should not be judged by serve alone; and, (2) He deserves a much more majestic moniker than Pistol Pete. By the time he's done, something like Peter the Great might be more appropriate.

Now a two-time Wimbledon champ, if Sampras continues to dominate the Grand Slams for the next few years, he surely will have earned the right to be listed in the section of the tennis annals reserved for the legendary few. And, yes, he also will have earned the right to be ranked among the game's royalty as, ahem, Peter the Great.

Already, the word "great" glides off the tongues of most fans and scribes when describing yet another sensational Sampras shot, which, by the way, might be executed from any part of a tennis court. From the baseline, he pounds great groundstrokes from both wings. At the net, he punches great volleys from either side and punishes lobs with great overheads. And, of course, he often powers past opponents with that goodness-gracious-great-balls-of-a-fiery serve.

"Pete Sampras is probably one of the most complete, one of the most talented, if not the most talented player out there," says Michael Chang. "He really can do everything: serve, volley, he can hit winners from the backcourt—and there are only a handful of players on the tour who can do that nowadays."

Sampras claimed the ITF Player of the Year award in 1993 by capturing a tour-high eight titles, including Wimbledon, where he defeated defending champion Agassi in the semifinals and Jim Courier in the final. Sampras also won the Lipton Championships as well as the US Open, defeating Alexander Volkov in the semifinals and Cedric Pioline, 6-4, 6-4, 6-3, in the final. He completed the year with an 83-15 record, becoming the first player since Ivan Lendl (1985) to win more than 80 matches.

He showed a champion's toughness at the 1993 Wimbledon by overcoming a serious shoulder problem, and a champion's touch and style at the 1993 US Open where, except for a quarterfinal battle against Chang, he effortlessly smothered the competition. Throughout his six-year career Sampras has proven to be a rarity among tennis superstars. He is a genuinely good guy who appears to have an awfully good game.

Pete Sampras, 1992. *Dom Furore/TENNIS*

"I'm not going to have an attitude like John [McEnroe]," Sampras says. "My image is that I'm a nice kid. I'm not going to throw a tantrum because I lost a match, because I know I'll be playing many more over the next 10 years."

With that very steady-as-she-goes approach to tennis (and life in general), Sampras is on course for a remarkable career. Last year, he became only the 11th player and fourth U.S. pro (joining Jimmy Connors, McEnroe and Courier) to be ranked No. 1 in the world since the computer rankings began in 1973. He began this year winning the Australian Open, defeating Todd Martin in the final. After falling to Courier in the quarters in Paris, Sampras sailed through the Wimbledon fortnight, knocking off Goran Ivanisevic for his second consecutive English title.

Says Sampras: "I like when people appreciate two guys who just go out and play tennis. I think that is the way tennis should be played, with class, by someone who doesn't lose his temper and embarrass himself."

Sampras' Wimbledon victory represented his fourth major title out of the last five Grand Slams and the fifth in his career. He took the No. 1 world ranking from Courier in April 1993, and by this June he held the largest margin over No. 2 (Michael Stich) of the computer rankings era.

"On his best day, I'd pick Sampras against anybody," says ESPN commentator Cliff Drysdale. "Before the 1990 US Open, all the other players used to say, 'Watch out for Pete.' Nobody knows how good you are better than the other players."

Sampras began playing tennis at age 7 and grew up admiring many of the great Australians, especially Rod Laver, winner of two Grand Slams (in 1962 and '69). Sampras changed from a two-handed backhand to a one-hander when he turned 16. That decision was essential in his development into one of the game's best serve-and-volleyers.

All the pieces finally came together for Sampras four years ago when Tim Gullikson became his coach. Gullikson taught him, among other things, baseline savvy and patience. The good-guy stuff was there before Gullikson came along.

"He's a great kid," Gullikson says. "He's the kind of guy most parents want their sons to grow up to be."

But he's not the kind of superstar/celebrity the media-types like to interview. Too controlled, not controversial and rarely gives great soundbites, the media cries. At Wimbledon in '93, Sampras did give the Brits one nugget of a soundbite, however. Upon being told that Princess Diana enthusiastically applauded his shots, Sampras said: "Maybe she has a crush on me."

When Sampras expressed "relief" after losing at the 1991 US Open, Connors questioned whether he had the hunger and confidence needed to be an all-time great.

Reflecting on his "relief" comment, Sampras says, "In 1990 I was very new to being a top player in the world and I had a tough time with that at first. But I'm more prepared to handle it now."

Though he understands that high visibility automatically qualifies him as a role model to many youngsters, Sampras said it's too soon for him to become immersed in global issues.

"I really don't think I'm going to get involved in any kind of political situations," he says. "I hope to one day do the kind of thing Arthur Ashe did, like going to jail for civil protest . . . but I'm still young. Maybe seven years from now there will be something I'll want to address. Right now I want to concentrate on winning tennis matches."

Despite the absence of a flashy personality—as in Agassi—Sampras's achievements and good-guy reputation have attracted several lucrative endorsement pacts. Nike (clothes and shoes), Bausch & Lomb and Movado watches are among his best.

But Pete Sampras seeks an even higher endorsement. Years from now, when the tennis gods take roll in that class reserved for the game's greatest, Sampras hopes to be seated front and center. He's certainly piling up the grades to get there. If the tennis gods take roll alphabetically, soon after Rod "the Rocket" Laver, ought to come Peter "the Great" Sampras.

Roger Federer and Tiger Woods, 2006. *Harry DiOrio/Getty Images*

IT'S SHOWTIME!

America—and the world, for that matter—waited anxiously as the calendar turned to a new millennium, not at all sure of what Y2K might bring. Happily, no catastrophe accompanied the dawn of the new decade; tragically, catastrophe of colossal proportion struck soon afterward. Still, the world of sports played a large part in the lengthy healing process, as the American population turned to the playing fields as an escape, a familiar respite in an increasingly unfamiliar world.

The US Open, with its New York soul ever on display, played a large part in that healing process simply by playing on. A special Opening Night tribute in 2002 honored the spirit and resiliency of the city and its myriad heroes. The event put on a grand show, a magnificent indication that it, like its host city, would continue to grow and thrive.

It was during this decade that the US Open truly developed its reputation as one of the world's greatest sports and entertainment spectaculars. It defined itself as the game's greatest show: world-class tennis, played before a worldwide fan base with an extra dash of world-class entertainment. It proved a recipe for success, as the US Open became the largest-attended annual sporting event in the world.

At the same time, the new century saw the US Open set the bar on innovation and make the event an experience unlike any other, by introducing a prime-time women's final, "US Open Blue" courts, electronic line-calling, giant video screens, letting fans keep balls hit into the stands and having winning players autograph tennis balls and launch them into the crowd. In this theater, the game's stars—including Andre Agassi, Roger Federer, Andy Roddick, Maria Sharapova and Venus and Serena Williams—somehow seemed bigger and more impressive. Perhaps everything seems more brilliant when it's played out on a great stage and illuminated by a Broadway spotlight.

And the show goes on. . . .

the CHAMPIONS

	MEN'S SINGLES	WOMEN'S SINGLES
2000	Marat Safin	Venus Williams
2001	Lleyton Hewitt	Venus Williams
2002	Pete Sampras	Serena Williams
2003	Andy Roddick	Justine Henin-Hardenne
2004	Roger Federer	Svetlana Kuznetsova
2005	Roger Federer	Kim Clijsters
2006	Roger Federer	Maria Sharapova
2007	Roger Federer	Justine Henin

Points in Time

2001 MEN'S QUARTERFINALS

Pete Sampras d. Andre Agassi,
6-7, 7-6, 7-6, 7-6

The rivalry between Andre Agassi and Pete Sampras spanned 13 years and 34 matches—including three US Open finals—yet this quarterfinal confrontation, played under the lights in Arthur Ashe Stadium, is considered their greatest match. Agassi was down a triple-set point in the opening-set tie-break but calmly collected six of the next seven points to claim the set. Back in another tie-break in the second set, Sampras punched an astonishing backhand reflex volley winner to even the match at one-set all. And then on they went to a third-set tie-break, which Sampras closed out with consecutive aces. The level of play was so high and error-free all night that the capacity crowd gave the pair a standing ovation at the start of the fourth-set tie-break, which Sampras won, 7-5. In four nearly immaculate sets that lasted three hours and 32 minutes, neither man lost his serve. Indeed, for Sampras, 30, and Agassi, 31, this match was one for the ages. ●

2003 WOMEN'S SEMIFINALS

Justine Henin-Hardenne d. Jennifer Capriati,
4-6, 7-5, 7-6

In front of a Friday night crowd at Arthur Ashe Stadium, Justine Henin-Hardenne (left) and Jennifer Capriati fought valiantly for more than three hours, raising the stakes time and again with dazzling shot-making despite a burdensome wind. Capriati served for the match at 5-3 in the second set and reached 30-30, only to be emphatically denied by Henin-Hardenne, who went on a four-game run to make it back to one set all. Capriati surged to 5-2 in the final set and again served for the match, but Henin-Hardenne worked herself out of one anxious moment after another—Capriati was two points away from winning on 11 separate occasions—and finally closed out the match at 12:27 a.m. on Saturday. That night, Henin-Hardenne summoned the strength to defeat fellow Belgian Kim Clijsters in straight sets for her first US Open title. ●

2005 MEN'S QUARTERFINALS

Andre Agassi d. James Blake,
3-6, 3-6, 6-3, 6-3, 7-6

Playing in his 20th consecutive US Open, in a match that began in Arthur Ashe Stadium at 10:16 p.m., 35-year-old Andre Agassi turned back the clock. He erased a two-set deficit and then, with James Blake (left) serving for the match at 5-4 in the fifth set and his J-Block crew firing up the sell-out crowd, forced a decisive tie-break. The comeback was finally completed at 1:09 a.m., with Agassi winning the tie-break, 8-6. "What does the Open mean to you?" he was asked afterwards. "That's what it means," he answered, "what you just saw out there. There's no place like it. It's 1:15 in the morning, 20,000 people out there. Tennis won tonight. That happens here in New York." ●

the HIGHLIGHTS

2000 A giant video screen is mounted on the outside of Louis Armstrong Stadium. This addition coincides with a big push to make the US Open a sports and entertainment spectacular, with stars from music, stage and screen performing throughout the event. ● Five years after playing what is believed to be her last US Open match, Martina Navratilova is back and playing women's doubles. In so doing, she becomes the only player to compete in all three main stadiums at the US Open. ● Todd Martin completes a two-sets-to-love comeback at 1:22 a.m. to defeat Carlos Moya in five sets—and then laps center court to exchange high-fives with die-hard fans who stayed for the entire match. ● President Bill Clinton (left) attends the women's final, becoming the first sitting U.S. president to attend the tournament. ● Venus Williams defeats Lindsay Davenport in the women's final, 6-4, 7-5, for her first US Open title. ● Marat Safin stuns Pete Sampras with a dominating victory in the men's final, 6-4, 6-3, 6-3.

The Road to the US Open

It's summer's ultimate reality series. World-class athletes relentlessly pursuing each other from town to town . . . tracing a path across North America that would make Rand McNally dizzy . . . their trek winding through two countries over eight weeks . . . leading to a grand finale in New York.

Since 2004, the world's top players have been gearing up for the US Open by competing in the Olympus US Open Series—the eight-week summer tennis season that links 10 North American tournaments to the sport's ultimate Grand Slam event, the US Open. Bonus points based on performance are awarded at each stop on the Olympus US Open Series,

with the top three men's and women's finishers in position to earn bonus prize money at the US Open.

In 2005, Kim Clijsters won $2.2 million—the largest payout in women's sports history—by virtue of her first-place finish in the Olympus US Open Series and her victory at the 2005 US Open. Roger Federer accomplished a similar feat in 2007, capturing both the Olympus US Open Series and the US Open to earn $2.4 million, the single largest payout in tennis history.

For players and fans alike, the Olympus US Open Series has added sizzle to an already hot summer season.

2001 The US Open goes from 16 to 32 seeds. ● Giant video screens are installed inside Arthur Ashe Stadium. ● USOpen.org, the official tournament website, is launched. ● The US Open schedules its women's final in prime time on network television, the first Grand Slam to do so. ● A junior qualifying event is added to the tournament program, creating more opportunities for the next generation of stars to compete at the highest level. ● The 32nd edition of the Andre Agassi–Pete Sampras rivalry produces the match of the tournament—and arguably of the Open era—as Sampras wins with neither player losing serve in the match. ● Venus Williams (left) defeats younger sister Serena, 6-2, 6-4, in the first-ever all-sister US Open singles final. ● Lleyton Hewitt upends Pete Sampras in the men's final, 7-6, 6-1, 6-1.

2002 Nearly one year after the September 11 attacks on the United States that destroyed New York City's World Trade Center, the US Open honors the spirit and resiliency of New York and the U.S. with an Opening Night ceremony that features the Ground Zero "Heroes Flag" and a moving on-court tribute. ● The first-ever all-women's night session at the US Open is played, with Martina Hingis defeating Amanda Coetzer, Jennifer Capriati topping Meghann Shaughnessy and the doubles team of Hingis and Anna Kournikova defeating Laura Granville and Jennifer Hopkins. ● Due to rains during the previous day, a record 103 matches are played on September 3. ● Serena Williams avenges the previous year's loss to older sister Venus in the prime-time final and wins her second US Open singles title, 6-4, 6-3. ● Pete Sampras (above right) wins his fifth US Open singles crown and 14th career Grand Slam title, defeating Andre Agassi, 6-3, 6-4, 5-7, 6-4, in his final professional match.

A LEGEND LENDS HER NAME

In 2006, the home of the US Open was re-christened the USTA Billie Jean King National Tennis Center, in honor of the legendary champion and pioneer. It was an altogether fitting tribute, as the world's largest public tennis facility now bears the name of the Hall of Famer and courageous crusader who began playing tennis in the public parks of Southern California and always has been one of the game's greatest ambassadors.

"Mi casa es su casa," said Billie Jean King at the conclusion of a moving dedication ceremony on Opening Night of the 2006 event. And indeed, King's house is open for all to enjoy, both as fans and as players. ●

A TORRENT OF TALENT

Following two days of relentless rain at the 2002 US Open, the courts of the USTA National Tennis Center were suddenly drenched in talent.

On Sunday, September 1, rain made it possible for only one of the 12 scheduled singles matches to be completed. So when the skies finally let up on late Monday—a day when another 19 men's and women's singles matches were on the slate—fans were faced with the happy dilemma of having too many matches to choose from.

The courts were dried and play managed to begin at 6:18 p.m., with the scheduling backlog resulting in a cavalcade of stars throughout the grounds. In addition to Andre Agassi, Lindsay Davenport, Jennifer Capriati (left), Tommy Haas, Lleyton Hewitt, Andy Roddick (above left) and Pete Sampras facing their respective opponents in the three main stadiums, there was Kim Clijsters playing Amelie Mauresmo on Court 10 and Justine Henin facing Daniela Hantuchova on Court 11, among a host of other matches. Play didn't end until Younes El Aynaoui reached the quarterfinals by defeating Wayne Ferreira on Court 4 at 2:14 a.m.—the second-latest finish in US Open history.

The action resumed less than nine hours later, with Chanda Rubin nearly upsetting two-time defending champion Venus Williams in the day's first match in Arthur Ashe Stadium. As on the previous evening, 16 different courts were used to help keep the tournament on schedule—and were used again and again. By the time this ninth day of play was over, fans had been treated to a US Open record of 103 matches in a single day. ●

the HIGHLIGHTS

2003 The tournament begins with Pete Sampras announcing his retirement from the sport in an emotional on-court ceremony during Opening Night. ● Prize money for the singles winners reaches a record $1 million. ● The US Open Court of Champions is introduced. ● The US Open's first "four-day" match is completed as Francesca Schiavone defeats Ai Sugiyama. The two players went on and off the court seven times during four days of rain. The wet conditions cause the cancellation of the junior doubles championships and force a special Friday night session, featuring the women's singles semifinals. ● Justine Henin-Hardenne defeats Kim Clijsters in the women's final, 7-5, 6-1. ● Andy Roddick (left) defeats Juan Carlos Ferrero in the men's final, 6-3, 7-6, 6-3.

Court of Champions

The US Open married its past and present with the 2003 introduction of the US Open Court of Champions, which honors the greatest singles champions in the history of the US Open and U.S. Championships. Each champion defines the essence of talent and character required to win at tennis's ultimate proving grounds.

The inaugural class of Jimmy Connors, Chris Evert, Billie Jean King, Rod Laver, Bill Tilden and Helen Wills spanned the Golden era (1881–1967) to the Open era (1968–present), with additional players being inducted each year. The 9,000-square-foot outdoor pavilion features a complete listing of all U.S. singles champions since the competition began in 1881. ●

Changing the Game

When the US Open left behind the serene surroundings of Forest Hills for the hard courts of Flushing Meadows–Corona Park in 1978, a new era of tennis began. With that change, America's Grand Slam no longer belonged to the country club. It belonged to the country.

That change in venue set the tone for a tournament at which change has been a constant, a common thread sewing together four unforgettable decades of excitement and innovation. Over the years, the US Open has evolved into one of the world's premier sports and entertainment events. And many of the innovations that the US Open has introduced to Grand Slam tennis have not only played a part in the tournament's growth but have had a resounding impact on the sport as a whole. Tie-breaks. Equal prize money. Night tennis. Hard courts. Prime-time final. And, most recently, electronic line-calling.

With its long history of new ideas and forward thinking, no other event has played the big points better. ●

₯004 The Olympus US Open Series, the eight-week [sum]mer tennis season that links 10 North American tournaments [to th]e US Open, is launched. ● Svetlana Kuznetsova defeats Elena [D]ementieva, 6-3, 7-5, in the women's final, which is played on the [3rd] anniversary of 9/11 and sees both Russian finalists (left) pay [tribut]e in pre-match and post-match activities. ● Roger Federer [defe]ats Lleyton Hewitt, 6-0, 7-6, 6-0, to win his first US Open [men']s title.

2005 "US Open Blue" tennis courts make their debut at the US Open. ● The facility unveils a hand-operated drawboard atop Louis Armstrong Stadium and two fountains in the South Plaza. ● Fans in Arthur Ashe Stadium who catch a match ball can keep it as a souvenir. ● Day turns to night as the final three matches in Arthur Ashe Stadium go the distance. The action concludes with Andre Agassi rallying from a two-set deficit to defeat James Blake. ● The US Open Wheelchair Competition (left) is introduced. ● Kim Clijsters collects a $2.2 million paycheck—the largest prize in women's sports history—for winning the Olympus US Open Series and then capturing the US Open women's title, by defeating Mary Pierce, 6-3, 6-1. ● Roger Federer defends his US Open men's title by defeating Andre Agassi, 6-3, 2-6, 7-6, 6-1.

Oscar and the Open

If you're into star gazing, there's no better place to look for luminaries than the US Open. Not only are the courts of the USTA Billie Jean King National Tennis Center teaming with the top talent in the pro game, but the stands are often populated with the top names in music, politics and entertainment—including an all-star cast of Academy Award winners.

Hilary Swank

Barbra Streisand

Jack Nicholson

Faye Dunaway

Holly Hunter

Sally Field

Nicole Kidman

the HIGHLIGHTS

2006 The USTA National Tennis Center is renamed for Billie Jean King during the Opening Night ceremony. Instant replay debuts in the main stadiums, with Mardy Fish being the first player to challenge a call in Grand Slam tournament history. Andre Agassi defeats Marcos Baghdatis in five thrilling sets in the second round before losing in the final match of his career to Benjamin Becker. After the match, Agassi receives a thundering ovation from the crowd—and then receives a second standing ovation, from the players, when he enters the locker room. Maria Sharapova (left) defeats Justine Henin-Hardenne in the women's final, 6-4, 6-4. Martina Navratilova teams with Bob Bryan to win the mixed doubles title in her final Grand Slam match. Roger Federer becomes the first man ever to win back-to-back Wimbledon and US Open titles for three straight years when he defeats Andy Roddick in the men's final, 6-2, 4-6, 7-5, 6-1.

Liza Minnelli

Dustin Hoffman

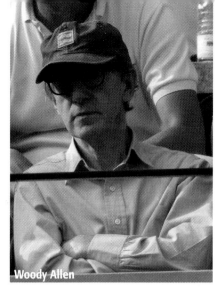
Woody Allen

Charlize Theron

Helen Hunt

Robin Williams

Kirk Douglas

Catherine Zeta-Jones and Michael Douglas

Robert DeNiro

2007 Two consecutive weeks of perfect weather help the total attendance top 700,000 for the first time ever. ● An open casting call launches a new tradition of having kids sing the national anthem and other patriotic songs in Arthur Ashe Stadium during each evening session. ● The 50th anniversary of Althea Gibson's first U.S. singles title is celebrated in an opening ceremony. ● Justine Henin wins her second US Open title by defeating Svetlana Kuznetsova in the women's final, 6-1, 6-3. ● Roger Federer (right) becomes the first man in the Open era to win four consecutive US Open titles—and collects $2.4 million, the largest payout in tennis history, for winning the Olympus US Open Series and capturing the US Open by defeating Novak Djokovic in the men's final, 7-6, 7-6, 6-4.

Arthur Ashe Stadium, 2007. *Art Seitz*

A FAMILY AFFAIR

by Joel Drucker

Serena Williams, the 1999 US Open champion, and Venus Williams, winner of the 2000 US Open, made the 2001 US Open women's final—the first to be held in prime time—a historic sister act. Joel Drucker reflected on the extraordinary accomplishments of the two siblings in the November/December 2001 issue of USTA Magazine.

THE FOLKLORE REMAINS VIVID. The tennis journey had started for Venus and Serena Williams on a garbage-strewn, stark hard court in Compton, Calif.

Of course, it had really begun when Richard Williams watched pro Virginia Ruzici hoist a big check after winning a tournament, at which point Richard decided he wanted to sire two athletes. Following Compton, the Williams' ride had continued to Florida, where the two sisters, eschewing junior competition, honed their games under the guidance of Jennifer Capriati's former coach, Rick Macci. Then, it was on to the pro tour, where the sisters rapidly stepped into the spotlight, winning at singles and doubles—at least when they chose to play.

Now, here they were, on practice court P-2 on the second Saturday of the US Open fortnight, hitting with each other nine hours before entering Arthur Ashe Stadium for a historic women's final, which would be won by Venus, 6-2, 6-4.

As usual, the practice was cluttered, the same confab of tennis and business and cameras that had groomed them for that evening's prime-time broadcast on CBS. One of the Williams' business managers, Leland Hardy, was strolling across the court in a snappy white suit and hat. Hitting partners gathered up balls. As Serena hit overheads, father Richard kneeled next to the net, looking up at her and snapping photos. Watching the practice session through a window in the players' dining lounge, U.S. Fed Cup Coach Billie Jean King reflected on the incredible impact the Williams family has had on their daughters' tennis.

"They don't have institutional involvement from coaches and other forces, so the family's got to play a key role in providing support in everything," King says. "Venus and Serena have done it their own way. Their family is remarkably grounded. Richard is the guy who jolts them, and while that can seem odd, there's a balance they get from their mother, Oracene. She knows what to ask, what kind of intensity to demand and how to support them."

Then again, the notion of two world-class athletes coming from the same family is not foreign to King. Her brother, Randy, enjoyed a decade-long Major League Baseball career. "Who knows?" mused King as she waited to toss the ceremonial coin for the final. "If Randy had been a girl, maybe we'd have met in the finals."

What the Williamses have done is extraordinary—and yet, by now, so heavily publicized that it all seems as preordained as the annual introduction of a new line of cars. Yet consider: The last time two sisters met in a Grand Slam final was 1884. "Sisters are rivals," Serena says. "A lot of people in families fight. Not our family. I guess our fighting is done on the court."

Venus and Serena fight in a vastly different era, an era where the line between sport and entertainment has been blurred, if not altogether erased. This final was in front of a huge TV audience of 22.7 million and a prime-time crowd that filled Arthur Ashe Stadium and included such celebrity attendees as Spike Lee, Diana Ross, Bruce Willis and Robert Redford. "People like to watch good entertainment," Serena says. "I wouldn't have missed it either if I knew something so historic was happening."

"I think definitely we're the top story in tennis," Venus says. "It's real exciting because every time I go out there—especially if I'm playing someone like Lindsay, Martina, Serena, Jennifer, Monica—I'm going to be in for a battle. That's exciting; good for all of us and for the sport, too."

Venus Williams, 2000. *Bob Kenas*

Serena Williams, 2001. *Carol Newsom/AFP/Getty Images*

Peel away the glitter, though, and you'll see that the sisters have taken strides not just as icons, but also as players. Venus and Serena sealed their role as cultural figures years ago. Fame earned them riches, but it also generated an increasing spirit of resentment among tennis insiders, a sense that Venus and Serena were more concerned with fashion than forehands.

"I decided I was going to become a competitor," Venus said during the US Open. Over the last two years, she has lived up to her word. Her forehand has improved considerably. Her movement, terrific from the outset, has consolidated into a more efficient series of patterns. Her serve, save for the occasional sputter, is the best in women's tennis. Her concentration is remarkable.

"She knows how to play points well, and that's not always easy to teach," King says. Her successful Open defense boosted her into company with Martina Navratilova and Steffi Graf as the only women players to win both Wimbledon and the US Open in consecutive years.

Increasingly gracious, Venus's maturity is rapidly overshadowing her father's antics. "When I was younger, I played tennis because my parents wanted me to," she says. "I suppose as I got older and I kind of understood what was going on around me, that's when I decided I wanted to be a player."

In 2002, Venus plans to play more tournaments in the early part of the year in hopes of generating ranking points to become No. 1. Motivated by Venus, Serena might well play more, too, even though she and Venus have rarely played singles in the same events save for Slams.

Serena also is trying to improve her game, mostly by taking advantage of the ease with which she can charge forward and the way her great balance and movement makes her a sharp volleyer. Both sisters are learning more to use their speed for offensive forays rather than defensive scrambling.

Bizarre as the Williams' path has always been, as much havoc as Richard has always wrought with his eccentric behavior, the truth is that the sisters have delivered the goods. Can they fulfill his prediction of becoming the top two players in tennis? Certainly Venus now rules the world, and if each sister plays more, it might well happen.

But it's also intriguing to see how effectively Venus and Serena would consistently perform if they indeed committed to a full schedule—including meeting one another at non-Slam events and regularly mixing it up against the game's best.

Still, the US Open showed just how much these two have raised the bar for the entire sport—both off and on the court. You really can't fake it in sports.

Rafael Nadal, 2007. *Timothy A. Clary/AFP/Getty Images*

Bob and Mike Bryan, 2007. *Matthew Stockman/Getty Images*

A FITTING FINALE

by Mark Preston

In 2006, after playing for 21 years, Andre Agassi closed his career on the great stage of the US Open. Mark Preston looked back in the September/October 2006 issue of USTA Magazine *on the star who shined his brightest whenever he took the court in New York.*

WHERE ELSE WOULD IT END? Where else could it end? What more perfect conclusion could there be to the Magical Mystery Tour that has been the career of Andre Agassi than one final bow on the great stage of the US Open? A career—a life, really—come full circle. Bigger-than-life, bold, brash, explosive in style and personality, Andre Agassi swaggered into the US Open as a 16-year-old phenom with big hair, a bigger forehand and an enormous presence. The Open—and tennis, for that matter—would never be the same.

As hard as it may be to believe for those of us who still have a vague idea of the whereabouts of our denim shorts, Agassi's US Open debut was 20 summers ago. When he steps onto the hard floor of Arthur Ashe Stadium this year, Agassi will be playing his 21st consecutive US Open. That, in itself, is a staggering feat.

But to gauge Agassi's impact on the US Open—or the Open's impact on Agassi—merely in measure of longevity would be to miss many big points. No, this is not the place where he won his first Grand Slam title; that would be Wimbledon in 1992. Neither is this the spot where he's won his most Grand Slam titles. Twice a winner here, he has won twice as many times at the Aussie Open. But the connection between Agassi and the US Open isn't about "first," or about "most." It's about those things that last.

Over the course of these two unforgettable decades, both Agassi and the Open have defined—and redefined—themselves any number of times. Each has often been an integral part of the other's growth.

Each has impacted and left an indelible mark on the other. Maybe it's because all of the aforementioned adjectives that define Agassi also define the Open. Whatever the reason, this much is for sure: This is Agassi's place, his event, his crowd. Others may have won more, but few have meant more.

Agassi understood, from the start, what a New York stage is all about. On so many occasions and on so many levels, he has delivered the spectacular, the singular sort of magic that only can be found in Flushing, and even then, only can be produced by the most remarkable of prestidigitators.

It didn't take long for that magic to begin. New Yorkers love the swagger, love those who can put it on the line and then back it up. And two first-round losses in his first two years here did nothing to shake Agassi's confidence or belief that he belonged. After his 1988 straight-set quarterfinal win over Jimmy Connors—their first-ever meeting in a Grand Slam event—18-year-old Agassi allowed that the match had gone pretty much as he'd expected, only that he figured the nine games he'd allowed Connors might have been differently distributed. "I predicted to a buddy that it would be 3, 3 and 3," said Agassi.

The media ate it up, and Connors got fired up. "He shouldn't say things like that because I'll be playing him again," said Connors. "He just made a bad mistake, which I'll remember." Agassi lost in the next round, but he'd officially arrived.

And he stayed. He did again play Connors the following year, and this time it took him five sets to win en route to another semifinal run. A year after that, in 1990, he reached the final here for the first time and began, in earnest, what would become one of the greatest rivalries in the history of this sport. Pete Sampras won that match,

Andre Agassi, 2006. *Action Images/WireImage.com*

Andre Agassi, 2006. *Ezra Shaw/Getty Images*

the first of his record 14 Grand Slam singles titles, but even on that day, there was something about that pairing that suggested it would play perfectly on the New York stage. Like Bialystock and Bloom, Agassi and Sampras seemed mated to be feted, destined to take their ultimate star turn on Broadway.

The two met here four times, and all of those—including the three finals in which they went head-to-head—were won by Sampras. But the quality of those matches resonates still, hovers in the US Open air on thick summer nights. There was the 1995 final that Agassi lost after winning everything the entire summer. There was the classic quarterfinal in 2001; the definitive final-Sunday sort of showdown held, this time, on a Wednesday. And there was the final final for the two in 2002, ending a rivalry that had lifted both men—and this event—to sensational heights.

"Andre is the best I've ever played," said Sampras afterward. "Playing against him, those moments are great moments, because you know you're competing against the best."

Agassi's two titles here—in 1994 and 1999—were very different and yet very similar, each defining the essence of a champion in their own particular way. He played here in '94 as an unseeded player, after wrist surgery in '93 had sliced into his ranking. But the fact that there was no number next to his name mattered little, as Agassi spit out five seeds en route to his first Open title, the first unseeded man to win the U.S. title in 28 years.

"Andre's run in '94 was a great story," says Jim Courier, an Agassi contemporary and himself a four-time Grand Slam champion. "But not because he won as an unseeded player. I think Andre not being seeded was much more of an upset than him winning the tournament. We all knew he obviously had the ability to win.

"What was most impressive about that win is the fact that he battled back, because he could just as easily have walked off into another career at that time. But he chose the hard road. He put in the time, and he didn't fake it.

He didn't cut any corners and he started to maximize his ability, and winning the Open was his reward for that."

Conversely, Agassi's 1999 US Open win was an exclamation point on a career year in which he won five titles, including two Slams, became only the fifth man in the history of the sport to win all four Slams in his career, and finished the year ranked No.1. After Agassi came back from a two-sets-to-one deficit to defeat Todd Martin, he shared his feelings about his relationship with the US Open.

"I feel like New York, all the people here, have really made me feel like I'm at home," Agassi said. "They've watched me grow up, and it's hard not to care on some level when you watch somebody develop from a teenager who says and does a lot of the wrong things to a person who gets out there and appreciates the opportunities.

"This is the most special place in the world for me to play. I'm convinced of it."

"I think Andre has come to appreciate every single thing in his life," says Mary Carillo. "He's very introspective and reflective. Andre loves the process, and that's why he could just as easily be a guy flipping his own scorecards at challengers as playing at the US Open. Yeah, there were years when he squandered some chances, but now I think he gets it more than anyone gets it. Nothing is lost on him anymore, and I think that inside his head, he's processed all of his US Open experiences, and the reaction he gets from the New York crowd every time he walks out there means the world to him."

Agassi admitted as much in addressing the press after his instant-classic quarterfinal win over James Blake at last year's Open, saying, "People have asked me, what does the Open mean to you? Well, that's what it means— what you just saw out there. It's 1:15 in the morning, 20,000 people out there…there's no place like it. That only happens here in New York."

New York. Where else could it end? ●

Roger Federer, 2007. *Chris McGrath/Getty Images*

40 Champions

ARTHUR ASHE

His name synonymous with integrity, dignity and class, Ashe was a champion of extraordinary talent and a man of extraordinary grace. He was the first US Open champion, a standard bearer not only in his sport but in the larger world. One of tennis's greatest ambassadors, he was a man of principle and purpose who used his celebrity to raise the profile of myriad causes. Certainly, there are champions with more trophies, but few with more passion than the man for whom the US Open's grandest stage is named.

MEN'S SINGLES CHAMPION: 1968

VIRGINIA WADE

The first woman to become a US Open champion, Wade upset Billie Jean King in the 1968 final to take home the first of her three Grand Slam crowns. Her career spanned the end of the amateur era and the start of the Open era, but there was nothing ambivalent about the way the British-born, South Africa–raised Wade played tennis. Lean and elegant, she preferred to slash her way to the net and attack incessantly.

WOMEN'S SINGLES CHAMPION: 1968

WOMEN'S DOUBLES CHAMPION: 1973, 1975

ROD LAVER

The "Rocket" was a remarkable champion after whom subsequent generations of champions would model—and measure—themselves. Both of the Aussie's U.S. singles titles, in 1962 and at the 1969 US Open, secured for him the sport's ultimate achievement, the Grand Slam. He is the only man ever to accomplish that feat twice. An all-court threat with all-world class, the left-handed Laver set the standard for greatness in the men's game.

MEN'S SINGLES CHAMPION: 1962 (U.S. NATIONAL), 1969

MARGARET SMITH COURT

One of the women's game's all-time greats, Court won a staggering 62 major titles in her career, including five U.S. crowns. In 1970, she captured all four majors, scoring the sport's highest achievement—the Grand Slam. At the US Open that year, she won the singles, doubles and mixed—a rare "Triple Crown." Indeed, she is the only player to achieve the Grand Slam in both singles and doubles, having completed the doubles Slam in 1963. Clearly, the Australian-born Court was a tenacious and talented champion.

WOMEN'S SINGLES CHAMPION: 1962, 1965 (U.S. NATIONAL); 1969, 1970, 1973

WOMEN'S DOUBLES CHAMPION: 1963 (U.S. NATIONAL), 1968, 1970, 1973, 1975

MIXED DOUBLES CHAMPION: 1961, 1962, 1963, 1964, 1965 (U.S. NATIONAL); 1969, 1970, 1972

KEN ROSEWALL

The man knows as "Muscles" was a mighty force in tennis over the span of three decades, winning his first U.S. singles crown in 1956 and his second, at age 35, in 1970. The diminutive Aussie played a big game, featuring superb movement, punishing ground strokes and precise volleying. Not only was Rosewall a great champion, but he was also a grand ambassador for the sport.

MEN'S SINGLES CHAMPION: 1956 (U.S. NATIONAL), 1970

MEN'S DOUBLES CHAMPION: 1956 (U.S. NATIONAL), 1969

MIXED DOUBLES CHAMPION: 1956 (U.S. NATIONAL)

STAN SMITH

One of the decidedly dominant figures in the sport in the late 1960s and early 1970s, Smith won his first Grand Slam singles title at Forest Hills in 1971. A superb athlete, he was a fine doubles player, which helped him hone his especially lethal net game. The Californian spanned both the amateur and professional eras in the sport, leaving his mark on the game as one of its great champions and gentlemen.

MEN'S SINGLES CHAMPION: 1971

MEN'S DOUBLES CHAMPION: 1968, 1974, 1978, 1980

ILIE NASTASE

This gifted Romanian, it has often been noted, possessed more talent in his little finger than most people have in their entire bodies. Of course, it wasn't the little finger he often displayed. Supremely athletic, Nastase was also supremely unpredictable, capable of playing beautiful tennis before his temperament would get the better of him. But in 1972, he was undeniably spectacular, upsetting Arthur Ashe on the Forest Hills grass in a five-set thriller of a final—the first of his two career Grand Slam singles crowns.

MEN'S SINGLES CHAMPION: 1972

MEN'S DOUBLES CHAMPION: 1975

BILLIE JEAN KING

She always had poor eyesight and remarkable vision. Fiercely determined, highly competitive and supremely talented, she surely would have succeeded in any pursuit, but happily for the sport, it was tennis that she chose as a career. King was one of a kind, a champion of a sport and of countless causes. She put women's tennis on the map, then charted her own course toward greatness on—and off—the court. Her 39 major titles include four U.S. singles crowns. There never has been, and never will be, another like her.

WOMEN'S SINGLES CHAMPION: 1967 (U.S. NATIONAL), 1971, 1972, 1974

WOMEN'S DOUBLES CHAMPION: 1964, 1967 (U.S. NATIONAL); 1974, 1978, 1980

MIXED DOUBLES CHAMPION: 1967 (U.S. NATIONAL), 1971, 1973, 1976

JOHN NEWCOMBE

Powerful, athletic and supremely competitive, Australia's Newcombe played an attacking game that served him well on the fast grass courts of Forest Hills. A winner there in 1967 as an amateur, he returned to take the title again in 1973—this time as a professional. Regardless of his playing status, he had but one playing style—full speed ahead. The owner of an excellent serve, big forehand and precise volleys, "Newk" was a popular and classy champion.

MEN'S SINGLES CHAMPION: 1967 (U.S. NATIONAL), 1973

MEN'S DOUBLES CHAMPION: 1967 (U.S. NATIONAL), 1971, 1973

MIXED DOUBLES CHAMPION: 1964 (U.S. NATIONAL)

MANUEL ORANTES

The Spaniard's only Grand Slam singles title came at the 1975 US Open, the first of only three to be played on clay courts. A gritty, relentless baseliner who loved to mix it up in the dirt, Orantes put together a stunning string of wins en route to the Open crown, taking out Ilie Nastase, Guillermo Vilas and Jimmy Connors in order to seal the win. A big left-hander with a bigger smile, Orantes, thanks to his win, helped boost tennis's popularity in his own country.

MEN'S SINGLES CHAMPION: 1975

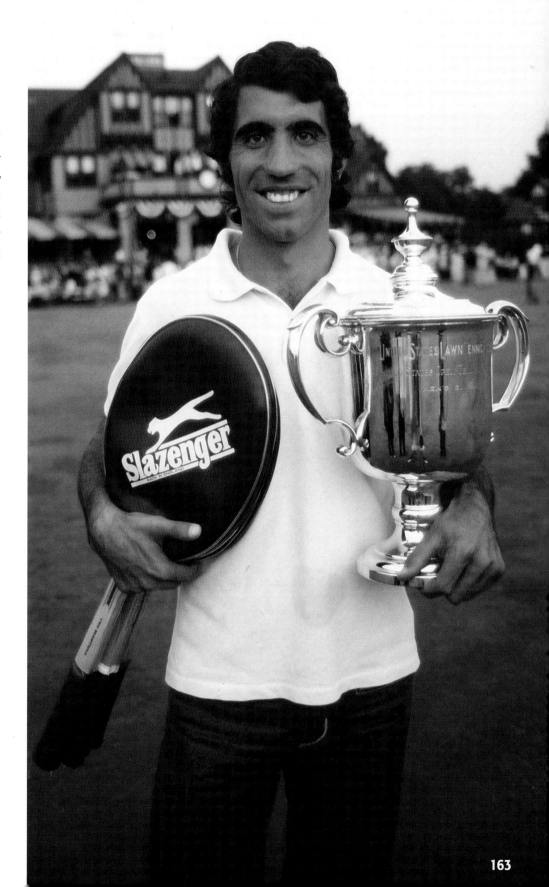

JIMMY CONNORS

No single player has ever defined the essence of the US Open better than Connors, who won five US Open titles on three different surfaces. Employing a two-fisted backhand that pounded foes into submission, he was a winner; but more, he was a fighter—and he enjoyed each and every fight. That made him a heavyweight fan favorite. Oversized ego, overboard personality, overwhelming talent—Connors was bigger than life, not unlike the tournament itself.

MEN'S SINGLES CHAMPION: 1974, 1976, 1978, 1982, 1983

MEN'S DOUBLES CHAMPION: 1975

TRACY AUSTIN

She was all pinafores and ponytails when she arrived at the US Open in 1977, belying the keen focus and killer instinct that she possessed. Austin was one of the most mentally tough champions ever to play the game, backing up her single-mindedness with a penetrating baseline game. It was a combination that won her US Open titles in 1979 and 1981—and won her a legion of fans as well.

WOMEN'S SINGLES CHAMPION: 1979, 1981

GUILLERMO VILAS

The Argentine strongman was a fan favorite wherever he played, and his 1977 surprise win over defending US Open champion Jimmy Connors at Forest Hills in the last US Open to be played on clay helped cement his legacy in the sport. The burly left-hander played a punishing baseline game, wearing down opponents through hard work and sheer will.

MEN'S SINGLES CHAMPION: 1977

CHRIS EVERT

She was America's sweetheart, winning over the New York crowd from the moment she set foot on the US Open's great stage in 1971. At 16, she roared to the semifinals, announcing her presence in the sport with a soft voice and thunderous game. Evert would go on to capture six US Open singles titles, compiling a remarkable 101–12 record at the event. On court, she was always the essence of cool, unleashing a two-fisted attack to which few could reply. More than a champion, she became an icon, the definition of greatness and grace.

WOMEN'S SINGLES CHAMPION: 1975, 1976, 1977, 1978, 1980, 1982

JOHN McENROE

The US Open was McEnroe's hometown tournament, and he always played like he owned the place. A supremely talented tempest whose personality overflowed the lines of a tennis court, he was equally at home on the singles and doubles courts, using a corkscrew left-handed serve to unleash his magnificent volleying skills and launch his attacking game. McEnroe has always been pure New York—bold and brash, talented and tough—and his star power helped illuminate the Open and give it the marquee status it now enjoys.

MEN'S SINGLES CHAMPION: 1979, 1980, 1981, 1984

MEN'S DOUBLES CHAMPION: 1979, 1981, 1983, 1989

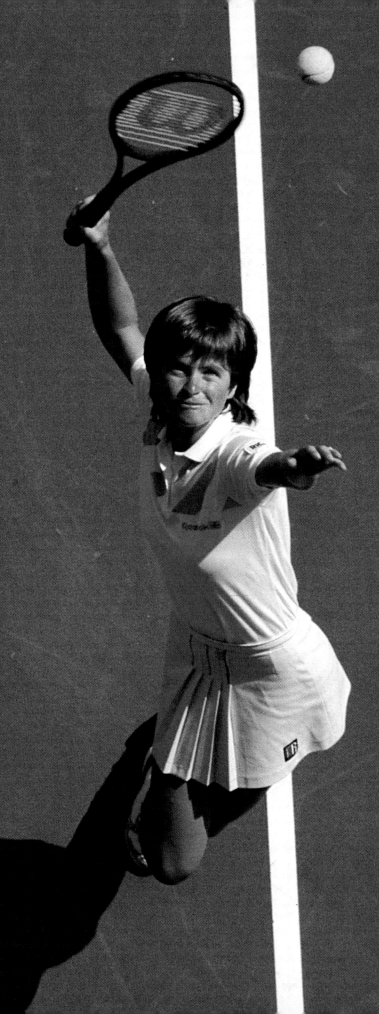

HANA
MANDLIKOVA

The talented Czech won her only US Open title on her third trip to the final, in 1985. That win, a back-and-forth three-setter over Martina Navratilova, showcased Mandlikova's superb shot-making ability, as well as her singular knack for out-attacking even the game's most aggressive attackers. She was supremely athletic, a player who loved to dictate play, charging forward at every opportunity. All told, she won four Slam singles titles and one Slam doubles crown—taking the 1989 US Open doubles title while paired with Navratilova.

WOMEN'S SINGLES CHAMPION: 1985

WOMEN'S DOUBLES CHAMPION: 1989

MATS WILANDER

The Swede was already wildly popular with New York fans by the time he captured his only US Open title in 1988, a year in which he won three of the four majors and ran away with the No. 1 world ranking. Wilander was at once quiet and yet charismatic, possessed of a certain charm and equally certain ability that played well on the New York stage. His five-set final victory over Ivan Lendl was a four-hour, 55-minute marathon—the longest US Open singles final in the Open era.

Men's Singles Champion: 1988

MARTINA NAVRATILOVA

Throughout a career defined equally by unparalleled longevity, unfailing brilliance and an uncompromising will to win, Navratilova epitomized the word "champion." Born in Czechoslovakia, but most assuredly made in America, she did nothing less than change the very face of tennis with an aggressive game and an unquenchable desire to be the best. Her four US Open singles titles are part of a résumé that includes 167 singles and 175 doubles titles, making her the most prolific winner in the history of the sport.

WOMEN'S SINGLES CHAMPION: 1983, 1984, 1986, 1987

WOMEN'S DOUBLES CHAMPION: 1977, 1978, 1980, 1983, 1984, 1986, 1987, 1989, 1990

MIXED DOUBLES CHAMPION: 1985, 1987, 2006

IVAN LENDL

Reaching the US Open final for eight consecutive years and winning three titles in a row, Lendl was the very definition of dominance. Tall and lean, and of Czech origin, he reshaped the men's game with a superior level of fitness and focus. His punishing ground strokes played superbly on the US Open's hard courts, and he backed up his game with a singular drive and determination to succeed. On court, he was all business—and that business was winning.

MEN'S SINGLES CHAMPION: 1985, 1986, 1987

BORIS BECKER

The German-born Becker played without fear, hurling himself into every battle, a blur of reddish-blonde hair, scraped elbows and bloody knees. His serve and his ground game were equally explosive, potent assault weapons on Flushing's hard floors. Thoughtful and introspective off court, Becker was reckless and demonstrative on court—a colorful contradiction and an electrifying champion.

MEN'S SINGLES CHAMPION: 1989

GABRIELA SABATINI

The graceful Argentine played a game that was beautiful to behold, an enthralling ballet of topspin ground strokes and tireless movement. Sabatini's 1990 US Open victory was her only career Grand Slam title, the culmination of a magical fortnight in which she defeated Steffi Graf in the final to become the first woman from her country to win a Slam.

WOMEN'S SINGLES CHAMPION: 1990

STEFFI GRAF

When she was on her game, there was little any opponent could do to stop the Graf juggernaut. The German moved beautifully and struck forcefully, pounding opponents with an awesome variety of weapons, none more lethal than her trademark forehand, which she could strike with remarkable power and equally impressive precision. Graf won five US Open singles titles, and in 1988 she swept all four majors and won the Olympic gold medal, scoring a "Golden Slam." Her 377 weeks at No. 1 is an all-time record.

WOMEN'S SINGLES CHAMPION: **1988, 1989, 1993, 1995, 1996**

PETE SAMPRAS

In a career that spanned three decades, Sampras rewrote the record books and redefined the word "champion." His quiet confidence, unfailing courage and unparalleled commitment to excellence defined him as a player and a person. Five of Sampras's record 14 Grand Slam singles titles were won at the US Open, including his first and his last. He will be recalled for his remarkable talent and inimitable class, and will long be remembered as one of the greatest ever to play the game.

Men's Singles Champion: **1990, 1993, 1995, 1996, 2002**

STEFAN EDBERG

The graceful Swede never really liked the US Open until he loved it, eventually learning to adapt his reserved personality to the decidedly unreserved pulse of the city and the event. With a quiet cool demeanor and an inferno of talent, Edberg won back-to-back US Open titles, proving the power of a positive attitude—and a potent volley. His hard-charging style was well suited to the Open's hard courts, where he always carried himself like a consummate professional and a true champion.

MEN'S SINGLES CHAMPION: **1991, 1992**

MEN'S DOUBLES CHAMPION: **1987**

MONICA SELES

Equal parts grunt, giggle and ground game, Seles became a dominant force in women's tennis in the early 1990s—a two-fisted slugger who knocked out opponents with a devastating mix of talent and tenacity. As delightful off court as she was dangerous on, she quickly became a US Open fan favorite, capturing back-to-back US Open singles titles in 1991 and 1992, and twice more reaching the final—in 1995 and 1996. Overcoming extraordinary adversity with exceptional grace, Seles proved herself not only a champion of a sport, but a paragon of the power of perseverance.

Women's Singles Champion: 1991, 1992

ARANTXA SÁNCHEZ-VICARIO

She was a bundle of unbridled energy, a study in perpetual motion and unparalleled glee. The fleet-of-foot Spaniard always seemed to be having fun, and that made watching her just that much more enjoyable. Twice a finalist at the US Open, Sánchez-Vicario captured the 1994 title with a win over Steffi Graf in the final, coming back from a set down to win in three. That win typified her persona—a fighter through to the final point.

WOMEN'S SINGLES CHAMPION: 1994

WOMEN'S DOUBLES CHAMPION: 1993, 1994

MIXED DOUBLES CHAMPION: 2000

PATRICK RAFTER

On the strength of his back-to-back US Open titles in 1997 and 1998, Rafter catapulted toward the top of the men's game. By 1999, the pony tailed crowd-pleaser was the No. 1 player in the world, the first Aussie to hold the top spot in the rankings since John Newcombe had similarly ascended in 1974. Beloved in his home country, Rafter—with his distinct serve-and-volley style and delight-ful personality—proved to be a New York fan-favorite as well.

MEN'S SINGLES CHAMPION: 1997, 1998

ANDRE AGASSI

Bold, brash and bigger than life, Agassi was a fan favorite before he had ever established his credentials as a champion. The kid from Vegas brought a full spectrum of color and charisma to the US Open, splashing its cement floors with his Technicolor attitude; big hair, big personality, big game. The New York crowd loved Agassi, and he them. In 21 years, he never missed a single US Open—proving himself the ultimate showman at the ultimate show.

MEN'S SINGLES CHAMPION: 1994, 1999

MARTINA HINGIS

The Swiss miss came to tennis with a game that was anything but neutral, winning three of the four majors in 1997, including her one US Open crown. Named for one of the game's all-time greats, Martina Navratilova, Hingis carved out her own share of greatness, capturing the No. 1 ranking by the age of 16. She owned a variety of potent weapons, but perhaps none as lethal as her poise in pursuit of the game's biggest prizes. She was absolutely unflappable, even at the youngest of ages, possessed of a vision that saw only victory.

WOMEN'S SINGLES CHAMPION: **1997**

WOMEN'S DOUBLES CHAMPION: **1998**

LINDSAY DAVENPORT

Growing up on the hard courts of Southern California, Davenport developed a game that was superbly fitted for the cement floors of Flushing Meadows. It was a game packed with power—big serve, big groundies, big volleys—a combination that usually brought large results. A former No. 1, she defeated another top-ranked talent, Martina Hingis, for her lone US Open title in 1998, won on her mother's birthday.

WOMEN'S SINGLES CHAMPION: 1998

WOMEN'S DOUBLES CHAMPION: 1997

MARAT SAFIN

Russia's Safin has always been an unpredictable player, and no one could have predicted the ease with which he captured the 2000 US Open title, slicing through the field and straight-setting Pete Sampras in the final. At only 20 years of age, the enigmatic star was dominant throughout his title run, picking apart opponents with a huge serve and relentless ground assault, breaking racquets and wills with equal aplomb.

MEN'S SINGLES CHAMPION: 2000

LLEYTON HEWITT

The fiery Aussie won his single US Open championship by running through a singular champion—Pete Sampras. On that day, Hewitt made an extraordinary player look downright ordinary, showcasing a blazing game that was equal parts firepower and footwork. A dogged fighter equipped with bold shot-making abilities from the backcourt, Hewitt plays a graceful game at breakneck speed, a sizzling sprinter with dazzling appeal.

MEN'S SINGLES CHAMPION: 2001

MEN'S DOUBLES CHAMPION: 2000

SERENA WILLIAMS

At the US Open, where the world's toughest tennis is played, no one competes more fiercely than the Williams sister known simply as "Serena." Her extraordinary will and powerful ground game are buttressed by one of the most potent serves in women's tennis. When in form, she plays only one way—in dominant fashion, with "dominant" and "fashion" being two words that can be applied to her in equal measure.

WOMEN'S SINGLES CHAMPION: 1999, 2002

WOMEN'S DOUBLES CHAMPION: 1999

MIXED DOUBLES CHAMPION: 1998

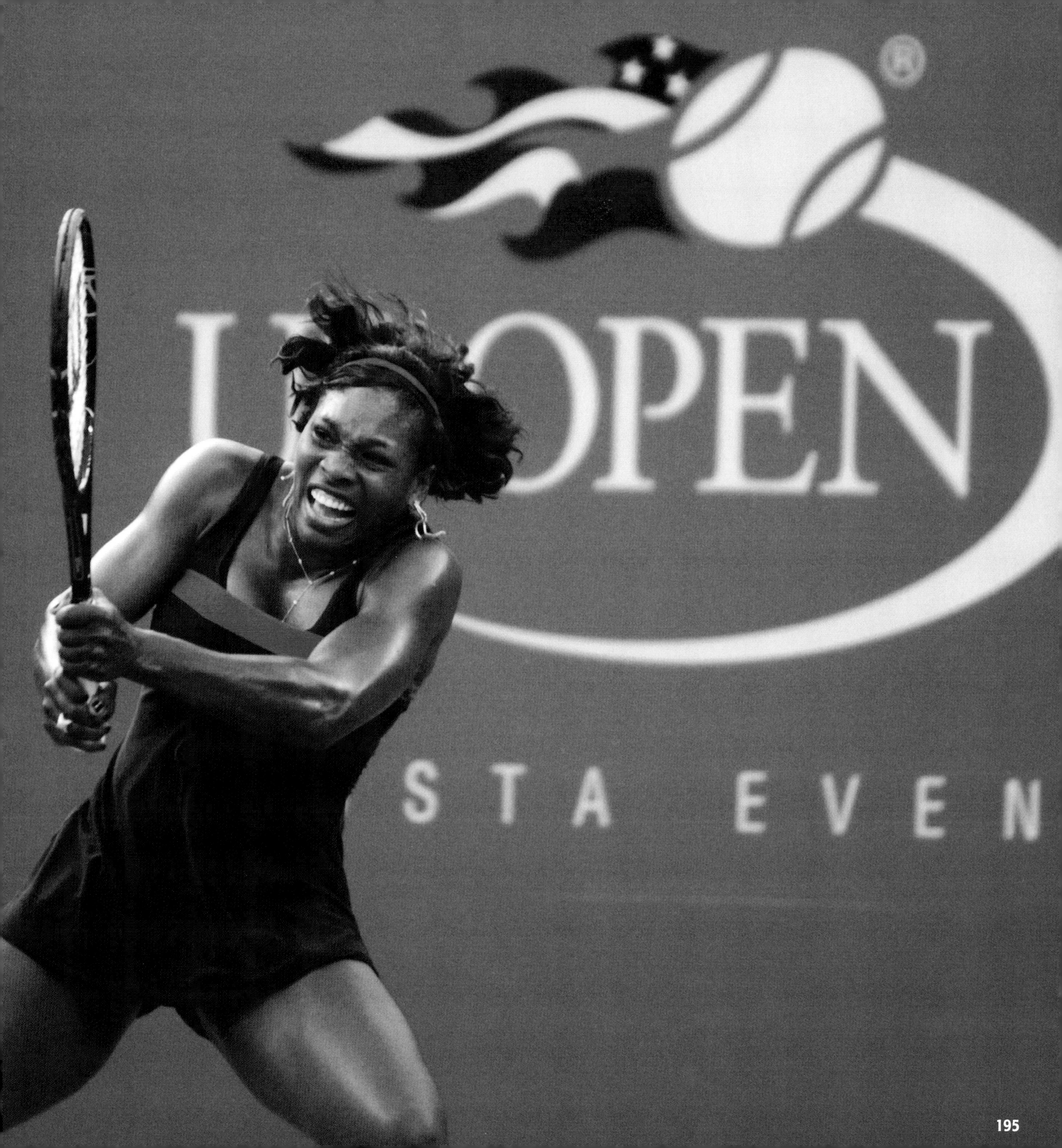
OPEN
STA EVEN

ANDY RODDICK

The 2003 US Open began with Pete Sampras saying good-bye to the sport and ended with Roddick introducing himself as the American heir apparent in the loudest way possible—by capturing his first Grand Slam title. Known for electrifying the New York crowd with his booming serve and lethal ground game, Roddick—always animated and often exuberant—has shown he knows only one way to play tennis, and that's all-out on every point.

MEN'S SINGLES CHAMPION: 2003

JUSTINE HENIN

Small in stature, with her trademark ball cap pulled low, the Belgian didn't, at first glance, seem an imposing presence. But on court, Henin played a large game, moving with the grace of a ballerina while blasting ground strokes that would knock the competition back on its heels. Her two US Open titles are testimony to her tenacity, as she out-played and out-willed her opponents with a sterling game and steely concentration.

WOMEN'S SINGLES CHAMPION: 2003, 2007

VENUS WILLIAMS

Right from the start, Venus has shone at the US Open as one of its brightest stars. As an unseeded finalist in her first US Open appearance, her auspicious debut in 1997 marked the beginning of a new era in women's tennis. She brought a new level of physical prowess to the game—affirmed by younger sister Serena—accentuated by tremendous court coverage, a sizzling serve and unrelenting ground strokes that have forced other players to train harder just to be on the same planet with Venus.

WOMEN'S SINGLES CHAMPION: 2000, 2001

WOMEN'S DOUBLES CHAMPION: 1999

KIM CLIJSTERS

The big-hitting Belgian won her only career Grand Slam singles title at the 2005 US Open. Having earlier won the Olympus US Open Series, she collected a record $2.2 million for her efforts—the largest prize-money payout in women's sports history. Supremely athletic, Clijsters covered the court like a blanket, hitting winners from all corners.

WOMEN'S SINGLES CHAMPION: 2005

SVETLANA KUZNETSOVA

Coming from a family of champion athletes, Kuznetsova has proved to be a champion herself. She arrived at the 2004 US Open among the least-heralded of the contingent of young Russians beginning to make their mark on the women's game. Yet in winning what turned out to be an all-Russian women's final, she became the lowest-seeded female player ever (No. 9) to secure the US Open crown, demonstrating that the overshadowed can sometimes be the most lethal of opponents.

WOMEN'S SINGLES CHAMPION: 2004

ROGER FEDERER

The Swiss star has redefined greatness on tennis's biggest stages and is the only man in the Open era to win four consecutive US Open crowns. He possesses the most fluid of games, an arsenal of weapons and an answer for every occasion; oftentimes what he does is incredibly hard, yet he makes it look so ridiculously easy. One of the greatest ever to play the game, Federer at the Open somehow always seems even greater.

MEN'S SINGLES CHAMPION: 2004, 2005, 2006, 2007

MARIA SHARAPOVA

If ever there were a persona tailor-made for the luminescence of the US Open, it is Sharapova, the Russian star who is equally at home before the cameras as she is on the court beneath the bright lights of Arthur Ashe Stadium. Here is a player who lives for the spotlight and has earned her place in it with a power game that can blunt even the most explosive of opponents. Her 2006 US Open win showed her as the picture of precision, a slugger of high style and equally high resolve. She should figure as a factor at New York for years to come.

WOMEN'S SINGLES CHAMPION: 2006

Arthur Ashe Stadium, 2005. *Matthew Stockman/Getty Images*